ORDER OF CHRISTIAN FUNERALS

Vigil Service

Evening Prayer

Leaders' Edition

ORDER OF CHRISTIAN FUNERALS

Vigil Service

Evening Prayer

Leaders' Edition

THE LITURGICAL PRESS
Collegeville, Minnesota

Nihil obstat: Rev. Robert C. Harren, J.C.L., *Censor deputatus.*
Imprimatur: ✢ Jerome Hanus, O.S.B., Bishop of St. Cloud. August 16, 1989.

ACKNOWLEDGMENTS

Excerpts from the English translation, from the general introduction, and from the pastoral notes, and original texts and arrangement of *Order of Christian Funerals* © 1989, 1985, International Committee on English in the Liturgy, Inc. (ICEL); excerpts from the English translation of *The Roman Missal* © 1973, ICEL; excerpts from the English translation of *The Liturgy of the Hours* © 1974, ICEL; excerpts from *Pastoral Care of the Sick: Rites of Anointing and Viaticum* © 1982, ICEL. All rights reserved.

Scripture readings used in this work are taken from *The New American Bible With Revised New Testament,* copyright © 1986 by the Confraternity of Christian Doctrine, Washington, D.C., and are used by license of said copyright owner. No part of *The New American Bible With Revised New Testament* may be reproduced in any form without permission in writing. All rights reserved.

Psalm texts are from *The Psalms: A New Translation* copyright © The Grail (England) 1963. Used by permission of G.I.A. Publications, Inc., U.S. agent.

Printed in the United States of America.

ISBN 0-8146-1503-1

Contents

INTRODUCTION

This book contains the rites and prayers of the *Order of Christian Funerals* which are intended for use by ministers before the Funeral Mass or Funeral Liturgy outside Mass: Vigil for the Deceased, Evening Prayer from the Office for the Dead, and Transfer of the Body to the Church or to the Place of Committal. It also includes selected readings, prayers for the dead, intercessions, and accompaniment for the music contained in the people's edition.

These services are arranged for celebration in the home of the deceased, in the funeral home, or in the church.

When the Vigil for the Deceased is celebrated in the church and is preceded by the reception of the body, the structure of the rite remains the same as that which is given here, except for the introductory rites, which are expanded to include: reception of the deceased at the entrance of the church and greeting, sprinkling with holy water, placing of the pall, entrance procession, and placing of Christian symbols. These rites are contained in the complete edition of the *Order of Christian Funerals,* pages 37–38 (nos. 82–86) and can be easily used with the people's edition for the Vigil, since none of the minister's texts requires a congregational response.

The rite for the Vigil for a Deceased Child has the same structure as that contained herein. Selected prayers and intercession are included in this book (pages 57–72). Appropriate readings for children, as well as other prayers and intercessions, are given in the complete edition, Part II (pages 139–147), Part III (pages 249–265), and throughout Part V.

The rite for the Transfer of the Body to the Church or Place of Committal may appropriately be used by a priest, deacon, or lay person before the body is brought to the church or cemetery.

Music should form an integral part of all the rites before the Funeral Mass or Funeral Liturgy outside Mass. Ministers are encouraged to make full use of the musical resources contained in this book.

Parishes are encouraged to experience the variety of music within this collection by expanding their ordinary repertoire. For example, some hymns in this collection may be used at Sunday Eucharist (taking care to respect copyrighted material); or some parishes may wish to prepare seasonal song leaflets in which music from this collection may be introduced to the parish. In addition, Psalm 27 and Psalm 63 in this collection are "Common Texts for Sung Responsorial Psalms," that is, they may be sung in Ordinary Time in place of the printed Sunday responsorial psalm (see *General Instruction of the Roman Missal,* no. 36).

The new *Order of Christian Funerals* envisions a diversity of ministers involved in the worship of the community, e.g., presiding ministers (priests, deacons, or, in their absence, laypersons*), cantors/song leaders, lectors, instrumentalists, the assembly itself. Good preparation for each service will include attention to these ministries. Readers are referred to "Ministry and Participation," paragraphs 64–68 of the *Order of Christian Funerals* (page 7 in this book).

Finally, a music ministry for funerals might be established, consisting of leadership given by local parish musicians, i.e., cantors, choir members, instrumentalists. For example, two cantors/song leaders might regularly lead the singing at Vigil Services or at Evening Prayer for the Dead when these are celebrated at the funeral home or in the home of the deceased. Or a special funeral choir might be developed, since the regular choir members may often be unable to attend funerals celebrated during the work week.

The event of death is one of sadness and of loss. But even as those left behind experience grief and anguish, they wish to be brought the hope and consolation of their faith. The careful pastoral use of the *Order of Christian Funerals*, the engagement of parish members and family in the carrying out of the services, and the prayerful celebration of the moments surrounding the death of a Christian assist the mourners to reaffirm their faith in the resurrection of the Lord.

> In the face of death, the Church confidently proclaims that God has created each person for eternal life and that Jesus, the Son of God, by his death and resurrection, has broken the chains of sin and death that bound humanity (General Introduction to the *Order of Christian Funerals*).

---

* "When no priest or deacon is available for the vigil and related rites or the rite of committal, a layperson presides" (General Introduction to the *Order of Christian Funerals*, no. 14).

VIGIL
AND RELATED RITES
AND PRAYERS

VIGIL
AND RELATED RITES
AND PRAYERS*

51 The rites provided here may be celebrated between the time of death and the funeral liturgy or, should there be no funeral liturgy, before the rite of committal.

These rites are examples or models of what can be done and should be adapted to the circumstances.

52 The time immediately following death is often one of bewilderment and may involve shock or heartrending grief for the family and close friends. The ministry of the Church at this time is one of gently accompanying the mourners in their initial adjustment to the fact of death and to the sorrow this entails. Through a careful use of the rites contained in this section, the minister helps the mourners to express their sorrow and to find strength and consolation through faith in Christ and his resurrection to eternal life. The members of the Christian community offer support to the mourners, especially by praying that the one they have lost may have eternal life.

53 Ministers should be aware that the experience of death can bring about in the mourners possible needs for reconciliation. With attentiveness to each situation, the minister can help to begin the process of reconciliation. In some cases this process may find expression in the celebration of the sacrament of penance, either before the funeral liturgy or at a later time.

*This edition is an excerpt from the complete *Order of Christian Funerals.* It contains the "Vigil for the Deceased," "Evening Prayer for the Dead," and "Transfer of the Body to the Church or to the Place of Committal." This last rite ("Transfer . . .") may be used at the funeral home as family and friends prepare to accompany the deceased to the church or to the place of committal.

The numbering of paragraphs corresponds to that of the Complete Edition.

VIGIL FOR THE DECEASED

Happy now are the dead who die in the Lord;
they shall find rest from their labors

54   The vigil for the deceased is the principal rite celebrated by the Christian community in the time following death and before the funeral liturgy, or if there is no funeral liturgy, before the rite of committal. It may take the form either of a liturgy of the word (nos. 69–81, 82–97) or of some part of the office for the dead (see Part IV, nos. 348–395). Two vigil services are provided: "Vigil for the Deceased" and "Vigil for the Deceased with Reception at the Church." The second service is used when the vigil is celebrated in the church and begins with the reception of the body.

55   The vigil may be celebrated in the home of the deceased, in the funeral home, parlor or chapel of rest, or in some other suitable place. It may also be celebrated in the church, but at a time well before the funeral liturgy, so that the funeral liturgy will not be lengthy and the liturgy of the word repetitious. Adaptations of the vigil will often be suggested by the place in which the celebration occurs. A celebration in the home of the deceased, for example, may be simplified and shortened.

If the reception of the body at church is celebrated apart from the vigil or the funeral liturgy, the "Vigil for the Deceased with Reception at the Church" may be used and simplified.

56   At the vigil the Christian community keeps watch with the family in prayer to the God of mercy and finds strength in Christ's presence. It is the first occasion among the funeral rites for the solemn reading of the word of God. In this time of loss the family and community turn to God's word as the source of faith and hope, as light and life in the face of darkness and death. Consoled by the redeeming word of God and by the abiding presence of Christ and his Spirit, the assembly at the vigil calls upon the Father of mercy to receive the deceased into the kingdom of light and peace.

STRUCTURE

57   The vigil in the form of the liturgy of the word consists of the introductory rites, the liturgy of the word, the prayer of intercession, and a concluding rite.

INTRODUCTORY RITES

58   The introductory rites gather the faithful together to form a community and to prepare all to listen to God's word. The introductory rites of the vigil

for the deceased include the greeting, an opening song, an invitation to prayer, a pause for silent prayer, and an opening prayer.

In the vigil for the deceased with reception at the church, the rite of reception forms the introductory rites (nos. 82–86). In this case the family and others who have accompanied the body are greeted at the entrance of the church. The body is then sprinkled with holy water and, if it is the custom, the pall is placed on the coffin by family members, friends, or the minister. The entrance procession follows, during which a hymn or psalm is sung. At the conclusion of the procession a symbol of the Christian life may be placed on the coffin. Then the invitation to prayer, a pause for silent prayer, and an opening prayer conclude the introductory rites.

The opening song or entrance song should be a profound expression of belief in eternal life and the resurrection of the dead, as well as a prayer of intercession for the dead.

LITURGY OF THE WORD

59 The proclamation of the word of God is the high point and central focus of the vigil. The liturgy of the word usually includes a first reading, responsorial psalm, gospel reading, and homily. A reader proclaims the first reading. The responsorial psalm should be sung, whenever possible. If an assisting deacon is present, he proclaims the gospel reading. Otherwise the presiding minister proclaims the gospel reading.

60 The purpose of the readings at the vigil is to proclaim the paschal mystery, teach remembrance of the dead, convey the hope of being gathered together in God's kingdom, and encourage the witness of Christian life. Above all, the readings tell of God's designs for a world in which suffering and death will relinquish their hold on all whom God has called his own. The responsorial psalm enables the community to respond in faith to the reading and to express its grief and its praise of God. In the selection of readings the needs of the mourners and the circumstances of the death should be kept in mind.

61 A homily based on the readings is given at the vigil to help those present find strength and hope in God's saving word.

PRAYER OF INTERCESSION

62 In the prayer of intercession the community calls upon God to comfort the mourners and to show mercy to the deceased. The prayer of intercession takes the form of a litany, the Lord's Prayer, and a concluding prayer.

After this prayer and before the blessing or at some other suitable time during the vigil, a member of the family or a friend of the deceased may speak in remembrance of the deceased.

CONCLUDING RITE

63   The vigil concludes with a blessing, which may be followed by a liturgical song or a few moments of silent prayer or both.

MINISTRY AND PARTICIPATION

64   Members of the local parish community should be encouraged to participate in the vigil as a sign of concern and support for the mourners. In many circumstances the vigil will be the first opportunity for friends, neighbors, and members of the local parish community to show their concern for the family of the deceased by gathering for prayer. The vigil may also serve as an opportunity for participation in the funeral by those who, because of work or other reasons, cannot be present for the funeral liturgy or the rite of committal.

65   The full participation by all present is to be encouraged. This is best achieved through careful planning of the celebration. Whenever possible, the family of the deceased should take part in the selection of texts and music and in the designation of liturgical ministers.

66   Besides the presiding minister, other available ministers (a reader, a cantor, an acolyte) should exercise their ministries. Family members may assume some of these liturgical roles, unless their grief prevents them from doing so.

The presiding minister and assisting ministers should vest for the vigil according to local custom. If the vigil is celebrated in the church, a priest or deacon who presides wears an alb or surplice with stole.

67   As needs require, and especially if the funeral liturgy or rite of committal is not to take place for a few days, the vigil may be celebrated more than once and should be adapted to each occasion.

68   Music is integral to any vigil, especially the vigil for the deceased. In the difficult circumstances following death, well-chosen music can touch the mourners and others present at levels of human need that words alone often fail to reach. Such music can enliven the faith of the community gathered to support the family and to affirm hope in the resurrection.

Whenever possible, an instrumentalist and a cantor or leader of song should assist the assembly's full participation in the singing.

In the choice of music for the vigil, preference should be given to the singing of the opening song and the responsorial psalm. The litany, the Lord's Prayer, and a closing song may also be sung.

OUTLINE OF THE RITE

INTRODUCTORY RITES

Greeting
Opening Song
Invitation to Prayer
Opening Prayer

LITURGY OF THE WORD

First Reading
Responsorial Psalm
Gospel
Homily

PRAYER OF INTERCESSION

Litany
The Lord's Prayer
Concluding Prayer

CONCLUDING RITE

Blessing

VIGIL FOR THE DECEASED

INTRODUCTORY RITES

GREETING

69 Using one of the following greetings, or in similar words, the minister greets those present.

A May the God of hope give you the fullness of peace, and may the Lord of life be always with you.

℞. And also with you.

B The grace and peace of God our Father and the Lord Jesus Christ be with you.

℞. And also with you.

C The grace and peace of God our Father, who raised Jesus from the dead, be always with you.

℞. And also with you.

D May the Father of mercies, the God of all consolation, be with you.

℞. And also with you.

OPENING SONG

70 The celebration continues with a song.

INVITATION TO PRAYER

71 In the following or similar words, the minister invites those present to pray.

My brothers and sisters, we believe that all the ties of friendship and affection which knit us as one throughout our lives do not unravel with death.

Confident that God always remembers the good we have done and forgives our sins, let us pray, asking God to gather N. to himself:

Pause for silent prayer.

OPENING PRAYER

72 The minister says one of the following prayers or one of those provided in nos. 398–399, pages 57–67.

A Lord our God,
the death of our brother/sister N.
recalls our human condition
and the brevity of our lives on earth.
But for those who believe in your love
death is not the end,
nor does it destroy the bonds
that you forge in our lives.
We share the faith of your Son's disciples
and the hope of the children of God.
Bring the light of Christ's resurrection
to this time of testing and pain
as we pray for N. and for those who love him/her,
through Christ our Lord.

℞. Amen.

B O God,
glory of believers and life of the just,
by the death and resurrection of your Son, we are redeemed:
have mercy on your servant N.,
and make him/her worthy to share the joys of paradise,
for he/she believed in the resurrection of the dead.

We ask this through Christ our Lord.

℞. Amen.

171

LITURGY OF THE WORD

> 73   The celebration continues with the liturgy of the word. Other readings, psalms, and gospel readings are given on pages 46–57.

FIRST READING

> 74   A reader proclaims the first reading.

A reading from the second letter of Paul
to the Corinthians   5:1, 6–10

We have an everlasting home in heaven.

We know that if our earthly dwelling, a tent, should be destroyed, we have a building from God, a dwelling not made with hands, eternal in heaven.

So we are always courageous, although we know that while we are at home in the body we are away from the Lord, for we walk by faith, not by sight. Yet we are courageous, and we would rather leave the body and go home to the Lord. Therefore, we aspire to please him, whether we are at home or away. For we must all appear before the judgment seat of Christ, so that each one may receive recompense, according to what he did in the body, whether good or evil.

This is the Word of the Lord.

RESPONSORIAL PSALM

> 75   The following psalm is sung or said or another psalm or song.
>
> [Here, the people's edition contains the music for the refrains of "Psalm 27: The Lord Is My Light" (no. 5, page 88), and "Psalm 63: My Soul Is Thirsting" (no. 8, page 90).]

℟. **The Lord is my light and my salvation.**

Or:

℟. **I believe that I shall see the good things of the Lord in the land of the living.**

Psalm 27

The Lord is my light and my help;
whom shall I fear?
The Lord is the stronghold of my life;
before whom shall I shrink?

℟. The Lord is my light and my salvation.

Or:

℟. I believe that I shall see the good things of the Lord in the land
of the living.

There is one thing I ask of the Lord,
for this I long,
to live in the house of the Lord,
all the days of my life,
to savor the sweetness of the Lord,
to behold his temple. ℟.

O Lord, hear my voice when I call;
have mercy and answer.
It is your face, O Lord, that I seek;
hide not your face. ℟.

I am sure I shall see the Lord's goodness
in the land of the living.
Hope in him, hold firm and take heart.
Hope in the Lord! ℟.

GOSPEL

76 The gospel reading is then proclaimed.

A reading from the holy gospel according to Luke 12:35–40

Be prepared.

Jesus told his disciples:

"Gird your loins and light your lamps and be like servants who
await their master's return from a wedding, ready to open immediately when he comes and knocks. Blessed are those servants whom

the master finds vigilant on his arrival. Amen, I say to you, he will gird himself, have them recline at table, and proceed to wait on them. And should he come in the second or third watch and find them prepared in this way, blessed are those servants. Be sure of this: if the master of the house had known the hour when the thief was coming, he would not have let his house be broken into. You also must be prepared, for at an hour you do not expect, the Son of Man will come."

This is the Gospel of the Lord.

HOMILY

77   A brief homily on the readings is then given.

PRAYER OF INTERCESSION

LITANY

78   The minister leads those present in the following litany.

Let us turn to Christ Jesus with confidence and faith in the power of his cross and resurrection:

Assisting minister:
Risen Lord, pattern of our life for ever:
Lord, have mercy.
Ry. Lord, have mercy.

Assisting minister:
Promise and image of what we shall be:
Lord, have mercy.
Ry. Lord, have mercy.

Son of God who came to destroy sin and death:
Lord, have mercy.
℟. Lord, have mercy.

Assisting minister:

Word of God who delivered us from the fear of death:
Lord, have mercy.
℟. Lord, have mercy.

Assisting minister:

Crucified Lord, forsaken in death, raised in glory:
Lord, have mercy.
℟. Lord, have mercy.

Assisting minister:

Lord Jesus, gentle Shepherd who bring rest to our souls, give peace
to N. for ever:
Lord, have mercy.
℟. Lord, have mercy.

Assisting minister:

Lord Jesus, you bless those who mourn and are in pain. Bless N.'s
family and friends who gather around him/her today.
Lord, have mercy.
℟. Lord, have mercy.

THE LORD'S PRAYER

79   Using one of the following invitations, or in similar words, the
minister invites those present to pray the Lord's Prayer.

A   Friends [Brothers and sisters], our true home is heaven. Therefore
let us pray to our heavenly Father as Jesus taught us:

B   With God there is mercy and fullness of redemption; let us pray
as Jesus taught us:

C   Let us pray for the coming of the kingdom as Jesus taught us:

All:

Our Father . . .

Concluding Prayer

80 The minister says one of the following prayers or one of those provided on pages 57–67.

A   Lord Jesus, our Redeemer,
you willingly gave yourself up to death,
so that all might be saved and pass from death to life.
We humbly ask you to comfort your servants in their grief
and to receive N. into the arms of your mercy.
You alone are the Holy One,
you are mercy itself;
by dying you unlocked the gates of life
    for those who believe in you.
Forgive N. his/her sins,
and grant him/her a place of happiness, light, and peace
in the kingdom of your glory for ever and ever.

    ℟. Amen.

B   Lord God,
you are attentive to the voice of our pleading.
Let us find in your Son
comfort in our sadness,
certainty in our doubt,
and courage to live through this hour.
Make our faith strong
through Christ our Lord.

    ℟. Amen.

A member or a friend of the family may speak in remembrance of the deceased.

CONCLUDING RITE

Blessing

81 The minister says:

Blessed are those who have died in the Lord;
let them rest from their labors for their good deeds go with them.

A gesture, for example, signing the forehead of the deceased with the sign of the cross, may accompany the following words.

Eternal rest grant unto him/her, O Lord.

℞. And let perpetual light shine upon him/her.

May he/she rest in peace.

℞. Amen.

May his/her soul and the souls of all the faithful departed, through the mercy of God, rest in peace.

℞. Amen.

A A minister who is a priest or deacon says:

May the peace of God,
which is beyond all understanding,
keep your hearts and minds
in the knowledge and love of God
and of his Son, our Lord Jesus Christ.

℞. Amen.

May almighty God bless you,
the Father, and the Son, ✠ and the Holy Spirit.

℞. Amen.

B A lay minister invokes God's blessing and signs himself or herself with the sign of the cross, saying:

May the love of God and the peace of the Lord Jesus Christ
bless and console us
and gently wipe every tear from our eyes:
in the name of the Father,
and of the Son, and of the Holy Spirit.

℞. Amen.

The vigil may conclude with a song or a few moments of silent prayer or both.

OFFICE FOR THE DEAD

OFFICE
FOR THE DEAD

348   The vigil for the deceased may be celebrated in the form of some part of the office for the dead. To encourage this form of the vigil, the chief hours, "Morning Prayer" and "Evening Prayer" are provided here. When the funeral liturgy is celebrated the evening before the committal, it may be appropriate to celebrate morning prayer before the procession to the place of committal.

349   In the celebration of the office for the dead members of the Christian community gather to offer praise and thanks to God especially for the gifts of redemption and resurrection, to intercede for the dead, and to find strength in Christ's victory over death. When the community celebrates the hours, Christ the Mediator and High Priest is truly present through his Spirit in the gathered assembly, in the proclamation of God's word, and in the prayer and song of the Church.[1] The community's celebration of the hours acknowledges that spiritual bond that links the Church on earth with the Church in heaven, for it is in union with the whole Church that this prayer is offered on behalf of the deceased.

350   At morning prayer the Christian community recalls "the resurrection of the Lord Jesus, the true light enlightening all people (see John 1:9) and 'the sun of justice' (Malachi 4:2) 'rising from on high' (Luke 1:78)."[2] The celebration of morning prayer from the office for the dead relates the death of the Christian to Christ's victory over death and affirms the hope that those who have received the light of Christ at baptism, will share in that victory.

351   At evening prayer the Christian community gathers to give thanks for the gifts it has received, to recall the sacrifice of Jesus Christ and the saving works of redemption, and to call upon Christ, the evening star and unconquerable light.[3] Through evening prayer from the office for the dead the community gives thanks to God for the gift of life received by the deceased and praises the Father for the redemption brought about by the sacrifice of his Son, who is the joy-giving light and the true source of hope.

[1] See General Instruction of the Liturgy of the Hours, no. 13.
[2] See General Instruction of the Liturgy of the Hours, no. 38.
[3] See General Instruction of the Liturgy of the Hours, no. 39.

STRUCTURE AND CONTENT OF
MORNING PRAYER AND EVENING PRAYER

352   Morning prayer and evening prayer from the office for the dead include the introduction (or the reception of the body), hymn, psalmody, reading, response to the word of God, gospel canticle, intercessions, concluding prayer, and dismissal.

INTRODUCTION VERSE OR RECEPTION OF THE BODY

353   Morning prayer and evening prayer begin with the introductory verse, *God, come to my assistance*, except when the invitatory replaces it, or when the rite of reception of the body is celebrated, since this replaces both the introductory verse and the hymn.

HYMN

354   To set the tone for the hour, a hymn is sung.

PSALMODY

355   In praying the psalms of the office for the dead, the assembly offers God praise and intercedes for the deceased person and the mourners in the words of prayer that Jesus himself used during his life on earth. Through the psalms the assembly prays in the voice of Christ, who intercedes on its behalf before the Father. In the psalms of petition and lament it expresses its sorrow and its firm hope in the redemption won by Christ. In the psalms of praise the assembly has a foretaste of the destiny of its deceased member and its own destiny, participation in the liturgy of heaven, where every tear will be wiped away and the Lord's victory over death will be complete.

356   Since the psalms are songs, whenever possible, they should be sung. The manner of singing them may be:
> 1. antiphonal, that is, two groups alternate singing the stanzas; the last stanza, the doxology, is sung by both groups;
> 2. responsorial, that is, the antiphon is sung by all before and after each stanza and the stanzas are sung by a cantor;
> 3. direct, that is, the stanzas are sung without interruption by all, by a choir, or by a cantor.

The rubrics for each psalm in morning prayer and evening prayer indicate a way for singing it; other ways may be used.

357   The psalmody of morning prayer from the office for the dead consists of Psalm 51, a psalm of lament and petition, Psalm 146 or Psalm 150, a psalm of praise, and an Old Testament canticle from Isaiah.

358   The psalmody of evening prayer consists of Psalm 121 and Psalm 130, two psalms of lament and petition, and a New Testament canticle from the letter of Paul to the Philippians.

359   For pastoral reasons, psalms other than those given in the office for the dead may be chosen, provided they are appropriate for the time of day and suitable for use in the office for the dead (see, for example, antiphons and psalms in the complete edition, Part III, p. 267).[4]

READING

360   The reading of the word of God in the office for the dead proclaims the paschal mystery and conveys the hope of being gathered together again in God's kingdom. The short reading in place in the hour or a longer Scripture reading from pages 46–57 may be used.[5] For pastoral reasons and if circumstances allow, a nonbiblical reading may be included at morning or evening prayer in addition to the reading from Scripture, as is the practice in the office of readings.

RESPONSE TO THE WORD OF GOD

361   A period of silence may follow the reading, then a brief homily based on the reading. After the homily the short responsory or another responsorial song (see, for example, no. 403 in the complete edition) may be sung or recited.

GOSPEL CANTICLE

362   After the response to the word of God, the Canticle of Zechariah is sung at morning prayer and the Canticle of Mary at evening prayer as an expression of praise and thanksgiving for redemption.[6]

363   During the singing of the gospel canticle, the altar, then the presiding minister and the congregation may be incensed.

INTERCESSIONS

364   In the intercessions of the office for the dead, the assembly prays that the deceased and all who die marked with the sign of faith may rise again together in the glory with Christ. The intercessions provided in the hour may be used or adapted to the circumstances, or new intercessions may be composed.

---

[4] See General Instruction of the Liturgy of the Hours, no. 252.
[5] See General Instruction of the Liturgy of the Hours, no. 46.
[6] See General Instruction of the Liturgy of the Hours, no. 50.

The presiding minister introduces the intercessions. An assisting minister sings or says the intentions. In keeping with the form of the intentions in the liturgy of the hours, the assembly responds with either the second part of the intention or the response. After a brief introduction by the presiding minister the assembly sings or says the Lord's Prayer.

Concluding Prayer and Dismissal

365 The concluding prayer, proclaimed by the presiding minister, completes the hour.

366 After the concluding prayer and before the dismissal a member of the family or a friend of the deceased may be invited to speak in remembrance of the deceased.

367 When the funeral liturgy is celebrated the evening before the committal, it may be appropriate to celebrate morning prayer before the procession to the place of committal. In such an instance the dismissal is omitted and the rite continues with the procession to the place of committal.

MINISTRY AND PARTICIPATION

368 The celebration of the office for the dead requires careful preparation, especially in the case of communities that may not be familiar with the liturgy of the hours. Pastors and other ministers should provide catechesis on the place and significance of the liturgy of the hours in the life of the Church and the purpose of the celebration of the office for the dead. They should also encourage members of the parish community to participate in the celebration as an effective means of prayer for the deceased, as a sign of their concern and support for the family and close friends, and as a sign of faith and hope in the paschal mystery. This catechesis will help to ensure the full and active participation of the assembly in the celebration of the office for the dead.

369 The office for the dead may be celebrated in the funeral home, parlor, chapel of rest, or in the church. In special circumstances, when the office is combined with the funeral liturgy, care should be taken that the celebration not be too lengthy.[7]

370 The place in which the celebration occurs will often suggest adaptations. A celebration in the home of the deceased, for example, may be simplified or shortened.

371 A priest or deacon should normally preside whenever the office for the dead is celebrated with a congregation; other ministers (a reader, a cantor,

[7] See General Instruction of the Liturgy of the Hours, nos. 93–97.

an acolyte) should exercise their proper ministries. In the absence of a priest or deacon, a layperson presides.

Whenever possible, ministers should involve the family of the deceased in the planning of the hour and in the designation of ministers.

The minister vests according to local custom. If morning prayer or evening prayer is celebrated in the church, a priest or a deacon who presides wears an alb or surplice with stole (a cope may also be worn).

372   The sung celebration of the liturgy of the hours "is more in keeping with the nature of this prayer, and a mark of both higher solemnity and closer union of hearts in offering praise to God."[8] Whenever possible, therefore, singing at morning or evening prayer should be encouraged.

In the choice of music preference should be given to the singing of the hymn, the psalmody, and the gospel canticle. The introductory verse, the responsory, the intercessions, the Lord's Prayer, and the dismissal may also be sung.

An organist or other instrumentalist and a cantor should assist the assembly in singing the hymn, psalms, and responses. The parish community should also prepare booklets or participation aids that contain an outline of the hour, the texts and music belonging to the people, and directions for posture, gesture, and movement.

---

[8] Congregation of Rites, Introduction *Musicam Sacram,* 5 March 1967, no. 37: AAS 59 (1967), 310; DOL 508, no. 4158.

EVENING PRAYER

OUTLINE OF THE RITE

Introductory Verse
Hymn
Psalmody
Reading
Responsory
Canticle of Mary
Intercessions
The Lord's Prayer
Concluding Prayer
Dismissal

EVENING PRAYER

385   When the celebration begins with the rite of reception of the body at the church (nos. 82–86) the introductory verse (no. 386) and the hymn (no. 387) are omitted and the celebration continues with the psalmody (no. 388).

INTRODUCTORY VERSE

386   All stand and make the sign of the cross as the minister says:

God, come to my assistance.
℟. Lord, make haste to help me.

Glory to the Father, and to the Son, and to the Holy Spirit:
℟. as it was in the beginning, is now, and will be for ever.
Amen [alleluia].

HYMN

387   The celebration continues with the following hymn, or another (see pages 98–121).

Lord Jesus Christ, abide with us,
Now that the sun has run its course;
Let hope not be obscured by night,
But may faith's darkness be as light.

Lord Jesus Christ, grant us your peace,
And when the trials of earth shall cease,
Grant us the morning light of grace,
The radiant splendor of your face.

Immortal, Holy, Threefold Light,
Yours be the kingdom, pow'r, and might;
All glory be eternally
To you, life-giving Trinity.

Text: *Mane nobiscum, Domine*, paraphrased by Jerome Leaman, copyright © 1980 Jerome Leaman.

PSALMODY

388   During the psalms and canticle,[1] all may sit or stand, according to custom.

---

[1] The method for singing each psalm and canticle as presented here is one way that may be used; other ways may also be used.

[The psalms and canticles should be sung. If they cannot be sung, they should be spoken slowly and reflectively.

A period of reflective silence follows each psalm.]

Boldface type signals the change of pitch for the flex (+), the middle (*), and the cadence.

FIRST PSALM—The cantor sings the antiphon and all repeat it. Two groups alternate singing the stanzas of the psalm; the last stanza, the doxology, is sung by all. The antiphon may be repeated by all after the doxology.

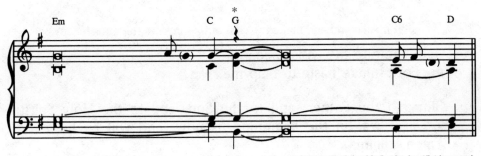

Psalm 121

Ant. **The Lord will keep you from all evil.*
He will guard your soul.**

Group 1:
I lift up my eyes to **the** mountains:*
from where shall **come** my help?
My help shall come from **the** Lord*
who made heav**en** and earth.

Group 2:
May he never allow you **to** stumble!*
Let him sleep **not,** your guard.
No, he sleeps not **nor** slumbers,*
Is**rael**'s guard.

Group 1:
The Lord is your guard and **your** shade;*
at your right **side** he stands.
By day the sun shall **not** smite you*
nor the moon **in** the night.

Group 2:
The Lord will guard you **from** evil,*
he will **guard** your soul.

The Lord will guard your going **and** coming*
both now **and** for ever.

    All:

Glory to the Father, and to **the** Son,*
and to the **Ho**ly Spirit:
as it was in the **begin**ning,*
is now, and will be for ev**er.** Amen.

    (a period of silence)

SECOND PSALM—The cantor sings the antiphon and all repeat it; the cantor
then sings the stanzas of the psalm and all repeat the antiphon after each
stanza.

    Psalm 130

ANTIPHON

If you, O Lord, should mark our guilt, ___ O Lord, who would sur-vive?

PSALM TONE

repeat for 6-line verse

    Cantor (reader):

Out of the depths I cry to you, **O** Lord,
Lord, hear **my** voice!
O let your ears be **at**tentive
to the voice of **my** pleading.

    Cantor (reader):

If you, O Lord, should mark **our** guilt,
Lord, who would **sur**vive?
But with you is found **for**giveness:
for this we **re**vere you.

ANTIPHON

If you, O Lord, should mark our guilt, _____ O Lord, who would sur-vive?

PSALM TONE

repeat for 6-line verse

Cantor (reader):

My soul is waiting for **the** Lord,
I count on **his** word.
My soul is longing for **the** Lord
more than watchman **for** daybreak.
Let the watchman count **on** daybreak
and Israel on **the** Lord.

Cantor (reader):

Because with the Lord there **is** mercy
and fullness of **re**demption,
Israel indeed he will **re**deem
from all its **in**iquity.

Cantor (reader):

Glory to the Father, and to **the** Son,
and to the Ho**ly** Spirit:
as it was in the **beginning**,
is now, and will be for ever. **Amen.**

(a period of silence.)

CANTICLE—The cantor sings the antiphon and all repeat it. Two groups alternate singing the stanzas of the psalm; the last stanza, the doxlogy, is sung by all. The antiphon may be repeated by all after the doxology.

Philippians 2:6-11

Ant. As the Father raises the dead and gives **them** life, *
so the Son gives life to **whom** he wills.

Group 1:

Though he was in the form of **God,** +
Jesus did not deem equality **with** God *
something **to** be grasped at.

Group 2:

Rather, he emptied him**self**+
and took the form of **a** slave, *
being born in the like**ness** of men.

Group 1:

He was known to be of human **es**tate, *
and it was thus that he hum**bled** himself,
obediently accepting ev**en** death, *
death **on** a cross!

Group 2:

Because of this, God highly **ex**alted him *
and bestowed on him the name above every **oth**er name,

Group 1:

so that at Jesus' **name**+
every knee **must** bend *
in the heavens, on the earth and und**er** the earth,

CANTICLE   29

and every tongue pro**claim**+
to the glory of God **the** Father:*
JESUS **CHRIST** IS LORD!

> All:

Glory to the Father, and to **the** Son,*
and to the **Holy** Spirit:
as it was in the **beginning,***
is now, and will be for ev**er.** Amen.

READING

389 All are seated during the reading. The following reading or one of those provided on pages 44–55 may be proclaimed by the reader.

1 Corinthians 15:55–57

"Where, O death, is your victory?
  Where, O death, is your sting?"
The sting of death is sin, and the power of sin is the law. But thanks be to God who gives us victory through our Lord Jesus Christ.

After the reading a period of silence may be observed; this may be followed by a brief homily.

RESPONSORY

390 One of the following responsories is then said.

A   Cantor or reader:

In you, Lord, is our hope. We shall never hope in vain.
R̄. In you, Lord, is our hope. We shall never hope in vain.

Cantor or reader:

We shall be glad and rejoice in your mercy.
R̄. We shall never hope in vain.

Cantor or reader:

Glory to the Father, and to the Son, and to the Holy Spirit.
R̄. In you, Lord, is our hope. We shall never hope in vain.

B   Cantor or reader:

Lord, in your steadfast love, give them eternal rest.
R̄. Lord, in your steadfast love, give them eternal rest.

You will come to judge the living and the dead.

℟. Give them eternal rest.

Cantor or reader:

Glory to the Father, and to the Son, and to the Holy Spirit.

℟. Lord, in your steadfast love, give them eternal rest.

CANTICLE OF MARY

391   If evening prayer is celebrated in the church, the altar may be incensed during the canticle, then the minister and the congregation. All stand as one of the following antiphons is sung by the cantor and then repeated by all.

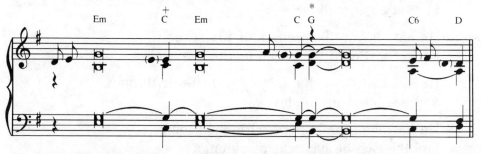

Psalm tone and accompaniment by Bartholomew Sayles, o.s.b. and Cecile Gertken, o.s.b. Copyright © 1983 by The Order of St. Benedict, Inc. All rights reserved.

Outside the Easter season:

Ant. **All that the Father gives me will come to me,** *
and whoever comes to me I shall not **turn** away.

Or:

During the Easter season:

Ant. **Our crucified and risen Lord** *
has redeemed us, **alleluia.**

All then make the sign of the cross as the canticle begins. The stanzas of the canticle are sung by all and the antiphon is repeated after the last stanza.

Luke 1:46–55

All:

My soul proclaims the greatness of the **Lord,** +
my spirit rejoice in God **my** Savior; *
for he has looked with favor on his **lowly** servant.

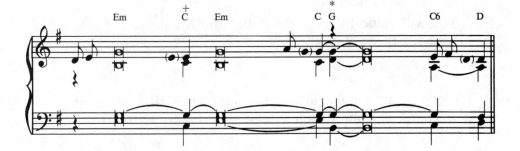

From this day all generations will call me **blessed:**+
the Almighty has done great things **for** me,*
and holy **is** his Name.

He has mercy on those **who** fear him*
in every **gen**eration.

He has shown the strength of **his** arm,*
he has scattered the proud in **their** conceit.

He has cast down the mighty from **their** thrones,*
and has lifted **up** the lowly.

He has filled the hungry **with** good things,*
and the rich he has sent **away** empty.

He has come to the help of his ser**vant** Israel*
for he has remembered his prom**ise** of mercy,
the promise he made to **our** fathers,*
to Abraham and his child**ren** for ever.

Glory to the Father, and to **the** Son,*
and to the **Holy** Spirit:
as it was in the **beg**inning,*
is now, and will be for ev**er.** Amen.

Outside the Easter season:

Ant. All that the Father gives me will come **to** me,*
and whoever comes to me I shall not **turn** away.

Or:

During the Easter season:

Ant. Our crucified and ris**en** Lord*
has redeemed us, **al**leluia.

INTERCESSIONS

392 The intercessions are then said. The following may be used or adapted to the circumstances, or new intercessions may be composed.

The minister says:

We acknowledge Christ the Lord through whom we hope that our lowly bodies will be made like his in glory, and we say:

℟. Lord, you are our life and resurrection.

Assisting minister:

Christ, Son of the living God, who raised up Lazarus, your friend, from the dead; raise up to life and glory the dead whom you have redeemed by your precious blood.

℟. Lord, you are our life and resurrection.

Assisting minister:

Christ, consoler of those who mourn, who dried the tears of the family of Lazarus, of the widow's son, and the daughter of Jairus; comfort those who mourn for the dead.

℟. Lord, you are our life and resurrection.

Assisting minister:

Christ, Savior, destroy the reign of sin in our earthly bodies, so that just as through sin we deserved punishment, so through you we may gain eternal life.

℟. Lord, you are our life and resurrection.

Assisting minister:

Christ, Redeemer, look on those who have no hope because they do not know you, may they receive faith in the resurrection and in the life of the world to come.

℟. Lord, you are our life and resurrection.

Assisting minister:

You revealed yourself to the blind man who begged for the light of his eyes; show your face to the dead who are still deprived of your light.

℟. Lord, you are our life and resurrection.

Assisting minister:

When at last our earthly home is dissolved, give us a home, not of earthly making, but built of eternity in heaven.

℞. Lord, you are our life and resurrection.

THE LORD'S PRAYER

393 In the following or similar words, the minister introduces the Lord's Prayer:

With God there is mercy and fullness of redemption; let us pray as Jesus taught us:

All:

Our Father . . .

CONCLUDING PRAYER

394 The minister says one of the following prayers or one of those provided on pages 57–67.

A God of loving kindness,   173
listen favorably to our prayers:
strengthen our belief that your Son has risen from the dead
and our hope that your servant N. will also rise again.

We ask this through our Lord Jesus Christ, your Son,
who lives and reigns with you and the Holy Spirit,
one God, for ever and ever.

℞. Amen.

B O God,   171
glory of believers and life of the just,
by the death and resurrection of your Son, we are redeemed:
have mercy on your servant N.,
and make him/her worthy to share the joys of paradise,
for he/she believed in the resurrection of the dead.

We ask this through our Lord Jesus Christ, your Son,
who lives and reigns with you and the Holy Spirit,
one God, for ever and ever.

℟. Amen.

C   During the Easter season:

Lord, in our grief we turn to you.
Are you not the God of love
who open your ears to all?

Listen to our prayers for your servant N.,
whom you have numbered among your own people:
lead him/her to your kingdom of light and peace
and count him/her among the saints in glory.

We ask this through our Lord Jesus Christ, your Son,
who lives and reigns with you and the Holy Spirit,
one God, for ever and ever.

℟. Amen.

   A member of the family or a friend of the deceased may speak in
   remembrance of the deceased.

DISMISSAL

   395 The minister then blesses the people.

A   A minister who is a priest or deacon says the following or another
   form of blessing, as at Mass.

The Lord be with you.

℟. And also with you.

May almighty God bless you,
the Father, ✠ and the Son, and the Holy Spirit.

℟. Amen.

B   A lay minister invokes God's blessing and signs himself or herself
   with the sign of the cross, saying:

May the Lord bless us,
protect us from all evil
and bring us to everlasting life.

R̂. Amen.

The minister then dismisses the people:

Go in peace.

R̂. Thanks be to God.

TRANSFER OF THE BODY
TO THE CHURCH
OR TO THE PLACE OF COMMITTAL

Your life is hidden now with Christ in God

119   This rite may be used for prayer with the family and close friends as they prepare to accompany the body of the deceased in the procession to the church or to the place of committal. It is a model, for adaptation by the minister according to the circumstances.

120   The procession to the church is a rite of initial separation of the mourners from the deceased; the procession to the place of committal is the journey to the place of final separation of the mourners from the deceased. Because the transfer of the body may be an occasion of great emotion for the mourners, the minister and other members of the community should make every effort to be present to support them. Reverent celebration of the rite can help reassure the mourners and create an atmosphere of calm preparation before the procession.

OUTLINE OF THE RITE

Invitation
Scripture Verse
Litany
The Lord's Prayer
Concluding Prayer
Invitation to the Procession
Procession to the Church
   or to the Place of Committal

TRANSFER OF THE BODY
TO THE CHURCH
OR TO THE PLACE OF COMMITTAL

INVITATION

121 In the following or similar words, the minister addresses those present.

Dear friends in Christ, in the name of Jesus and of his Church, we gather to pray for N., that God may bring him/her to everlasting peace and rest.

We share the pain of loss, but the promise of eternal life gives us hope. Let us comfort one another with these words:

SCRIPTURE VERSE

122 One of the following or another brief Scripture verse is read.

A　　Colossians 3:3–4

You have died, and your life is hidden with Christ in God. When Christ your life appears, then you too will appear with him in glory.

B　　Romans 6:8–9

If we have died with Christ, we believe that we shall also live with him. We know that Christ, raised from the dead, dies no more; death no longer has power over him.

LITANY

123 The minister leads those present in the following litany.

Dear friends, our Lord comes to raise the dead and comforts us with the solace of his love. Let us praise the Lord Jesus Christ.

Assisting minister:

Word of God, Creator of the earth to which N. now returns; in baptism you called him/her to eternal life to praise your Father for ever.
Lord, have mercy.
℟. Lord, have mercy.

Assisting minister:

Son of God, you raise up the just and clothe them with the glory of your kingdom:
Lord, have mercy.
℟. Lord, have mercy.

Assisting minister:

Crucified Lord, you protect the soul of N. by the power of your cross, and on the day of your coming you will show mercy to all the faithful departed:
Lord, have mercy.
℟. Lord, have mercy.

Assisting minister:

Judge of the living and the dead, at your voice the tombs will open and all the just who sleep in your peace will rise and sing the glory of God:
Lord, have mercy.
℟. Lord, have mercy.

Assisting minister:

All praise to you Jesus our Savior, death is in your hands and all the living depend on you alone:
Lord, have mercy.
℟. Lord, have mercy.

THE LORD'S PRAYER

124 In the following or similar words, the minister invites those present to pray the Lord's Prayer.

With faith and hope we pray to the Father in the words Jesus taught his disciples:

All:

Our Father . . .

Concluding Prayer

125 The minister says one of the following prayers or one of those provided on pages 57–67.

A Lord,
   N. is gone now from this earthly dwelling
   and has left behind those who mourn his/her absence.
   Grant that as we grieve for our brother/sister
   we may hold his/her memory dear
   and live in hope of the eternal kingdom
   where you will bring us together again.
   We ask this through Christ our Lord.

   R⁄. Amen.

B Lord, in our grief we turn to you.   33
   Are you not the God of love
   who open your ears to all?
   Listen to our prayers for your servant N.,
   whom you have called out of this world:
   lead him/her to your kingdom of light and peace
   and count him/her among the saints in glory.
   We ask this through Christ our Lord.

   R⁄. Amen.

C God of all consolation,   176
   open our hearts to your word,
   so that, listening to it, we may comfort one another,
   finding light in time of darkness
   and faith in time of doubt.
   We ask this through Christ our Lord.

   R⁄. Amen.

   The minister invites those present to pray in silence while all is made
   ready for the procession.

Invitation to the Procession

126   In the following or similar words, the minister invites those present to join in the procession.

The Lord guards our coming in and our going out.
May God be with us today
as we make this last journey with our brother/sister.

Procession to the Church
or to the Place of Committal

127   During the procession, psalms and other suitable songs may be sung. If this is not possible, a psalm is sung or recited either before or after the procession. The following psalm and others provided on pages 48–50 may be used.

℞. I rejoiced when I heard them say: let us go to the house of the Lord.

Or:

℞. Let us go rejoicing to the house of the Lord.

Psalm 122

I rejoiced when I heard them say:
"Let us go to God's house."
And now our feet are standing
within your gates, O Jerusalem. ℞.

Jerusalem is built as a city
strongly compact.
It is there that the tribes go up,
the tribes of the Lord. ℞.

For Israel's law it is,
there to praise the Lord's name.
There were set the thrones of judgment
of the house of David. ℞.

For the peace of Jerusalem pray:
"Peace be to your homes!
May peace reign in your walls,
in your palaces, peace!" ℞.

For love of my brethren and friends
I say: "Peace upon you!"
For love of the house of the Lord
I will ask for your good. R⁊.

If the reception of the body at the church is celebrated apart from the vigil or the funeral liturgy, the "Vigil for the Deceased with Reception at the Church" may be used and simplified (see complete edition).

SELECTED READINGS

Old Testament Readings

1   A reading from the book of Job   19:1, 23–27

I know that my Redeemer lives.

Job answered and said:

Oh, would that my words were written down!
   Would that they were inscribed in a record:
That with an iron chisel and with lead
   they were cut in the rock forever!
But as for me, I know that my Vindicator lives,
   and that he will at last stand forth upon the dust;
Whom I myself shall see:
   my own eyes, not another's, shall behold him,
And from my flesh I shall see God;
   my inmost being is consumed with longing.

This is the Word of the Lord.

2   A reading from the book of the prophet Isaiah   25:6a, 7–9

The Lord God will destroy death for ever.

On this mountain the LORD of hosts
   will provide for all peoples.
On this mountain he will destroy
   the veil that veils all peoples,
The web that is woven over all nations;
   he will destroy death forever.
The Lord GOD will wipe away
   the tears from all faces;
The reproach of his people he will remove
   from the whole earth; for the LORD has spoken.

On that day it will be said:
"Behold our God, to whom we looked to save us!
   This is the LORD for whom we looked;
   let us rejoice and be glad that he has saved us!"

This is the Word of the Lord.

345 During the Easter season, reading 1, 8, or 9 is used as the first reading instead of a reading from the Old Testament.

1   Shorter form:

A reading from the Acts of the Apostles   10:34–36, 42–43

God has appointed Jesus to judge everyone, alive and dead.

Peter proceeded to address the people in these words:

"In truth, I see that God shows no partiality. Rather, in every nation whoever fears him and acts uprightly is acceptable to him. You know the word that he sent to the Israelites as he proclaimed peace through Jesus Christ, who is Lord of all. He commissioned us to preach to the people and testify that he is the one appointed by God as judge of the living and the dead. To him all the prophets bear witness, that everyone who believes in him will receive forgiveness of sins through his name."

This is the Word of the Lord.

2   Shorter form:

A reading from the letter of Paul to the Romans   6:3–4, 8–9

Let us walk in newness of life.

Are you unaware that we who were baptized into Christ Jesus were baptized into his death? We were indeed buried with him through baptism into death, so that, just as Christ was raised from the dead by the glory of the Father, we too might live in newness of life. If, then, we have died with Christ, we believe that we shall also live with him. We know that Christ, raised from the dead, dies no more; death no longer has power over him.

This is the Word of the Lord.

3   A reading from the letter of Paul to the Romans   8:14–23

We groan while we wait for the redemption of our bodies.

Those who are led by the Spirit of God are children of God. For you did not receive a spirit of slavery to fall back into fear, but you received a spirit of adoption, through which we cry, "*Abba,* Father!" The Spirit itself bears witness with our spirit that we are children of God, and if children, then heirs, heirs of God and joint heirs with Christ, if only we suffer with him so that we may also be glorified with him.

I consider that the sufferings of this present time are as nothing compared with the glory to be revealed for us. For creation awaits with eager expectation the revelation of the children of God; for creation was made subject to futility, not of its own accord but because of the one who subjected it, in hope that creation itself would be set free from slavery to corruption and share in the glorious freedom of the children of God. We know that all creation is groaning in labor pains even until now; and not only that, but we ourselves, who have the firstfruits of the Spirit, we also groan within ourselves as we wait for adoption, the redemption of our bodies.

This is the Word of the Lord.

4   A reading from the letter of Paul to the Romans   14:7–9, 10b–12
Whether alive or dead, we belong to the Lord.

None of us lives for oneself, and no one dies for oneself. For if we live, we live for the Lord, and if we die, we die for the Lord; so then, whether we live or die, we are the Lord's. For this is why Christ died and came to life, that he might be Lord of both the dead and the living. For we shall all stand before the judgment seat of God; for it is written: "As I live, says the Lord, every knee shall bend before me, and every tongue shall give praise to God."

So then each of us shall give an account of himself to God.

This is the Word of the Lord.

5   A reading from the first letter of Paul
to the Corinthians   15:51–57
Death is swallowed up in victory.

Behold, I tell you a mystery. We shall not all fall asleep, but we will all be changed, in an instant, in the blink of an eye, at the last trumpet. For the trumpet will sound, the dead will be raised incorruptible, and we shall be changed. For that which is corruptible must clothe itself with incorruptibility, and that which is mortal must clothe itself with immortality. And when that which is corruptible clothes itself with incorruptibility and that which is mortal clothes itself with immortality, then the word that is written shall come about:

"Death is swallowed up in victory.
Where, O death, is your victory?
Where, O death, is your sting?"

The sting of death is sin, and the power of sin is the law. But thanks be to God who gives us the victory through our Lord Jesus Christ.

This is the Word of the Lord.

6   A reading from the second letter of Paul
to the Corinthians   5:1, 6–10

We have an everlasting home in heaven.

We know that if our earthly dwelling, a tent, should be destroyed, we have a building from God, a dwelling not made with hands, eternal in heaven.

So we are always courageous, although we know that while we are at home in the body we are away from the Lord, for we walk by faith, not by sight. Yet we are courageous, and we would rather leave the body and go home to the Lord. Therefore, we aspire to please him, whether we are at home or away. For we must all appear before the judgment seat of Christ, so that each one may receive recompense, according to what he did in the body, whether good or evil.

This is the Word of the Lord.

7   A reading from the first letter of John   3:1–2

We shall see God as he really is.

See what love the Father has bestowed on us that we may be called the children of God. Yet so we are. The reason the world does not know us is that it did not know him. Beloved, we are God's children now; what we shall be has not yet been revealed. We do know that when it is revealed we shall be like him, for we shall see him as he is.

This is the Word of the Lord.

8   A reading from the book of Revelation   14:13

Happy are those who die in the Lord.

I heard a voice from heaven say, "Write this: Blessed are the dead who die in the Lord from now on." "Yes," said the Spirit, "let them find rest from their labors, for their works accompany them."

This is the Word of the Lord.

9   A reading from the book of Revelation   20:11—21:1

The dead have been judged according to their works.

I saw a large white throne and the one who was sitting on it. The earth and the sky fled from his presence and there was no place for them. I saw the dead, the great and the lowly, standing before the throne, and scrolls were opened. Then another scroll was opened, the book of life. The dead were judged according to their deeds, by what was written in the scrolls. The sea gave up its dead; then Death and Hades gave up their dead. All the dead were judged according to their deeds. Then Death and Hades were thrown into the pool of fire. (This pool of fire is the second death.) Anyone whose name was not found written in the book of life was thrown into the pool of fire.

Then I saw a new heaven and a new earth. The former heaven and the former earth had passed away, and the sea was no more.

This is the Word of the Lord.

RESPONSORIAL PSALMS

1   Psalm 23

℟. The Lord is my shepherd; there is nothing I shall want.
    Or:

℟. Though I walk in the valley of darkness, I fear no evil, for you are with me.

The Lord is my shepherd;
there is nothing I shall want.
Fresh and green are the pastures

where he gives me repose.
Near restful waters he leads me,
to revive my drooping spirit. R⁷.

He guides me along the right path;
he is true to his name.
If I should walk in the valley of darkness
no evil would I fear.
You are there with your crook and your staff;
with these you give me comfort. R⁷.

You have prepared a banquet for me
in the sight of my foes.
My head you have anointed with oil;
my cup is overflowing. R⁷.

Surely goodness and kindness shall follow me
all the days of my life.
In the Lord's own house shall I dwell
for ever and ever. R⁷.

2   Psalm 116

R⁷. I will walk in the presence of the Lord in the land of
the living.

   Or:

R⁷. Alleluia.

How gracious is the Lord, and just;
our God has compassion.
The Lord protects the simple hearts;
I was helpless so he saved me. R⁷.

I trusted, even when I said:
"I am sorely afflicted,"
and when I said in my alarm:
"No man can be trusted." R⁷.

O precious in the eyes of the Lord
is the death of his faithful.
Your servant, Lord, your servant am I;
you have loosened my bonds. R⁷.

3   Psalm 130

℟. Out of the depths, I cry to you, Lord.

   Or:

℟. I hope in the Lord, I trust in his word.

Out of the depths I cry to you, O Lord,
Lord, hear my voice!
O let your ears be attentive
to the voice of my pleading. ℟.

If you, O Lord, should mark our guilt,
Lord, who would survive?
But with you is found forgiveness:
for this we revere you. ℟.

My soul is waiting for the Lord,
I count on his word.
My soul is longing for the Lord
more than watchman for daybreak. ℟.

Because with the Lord there is mercy
and fullness of redemption,
Israel indeed he will redeem
from all its iniquity. ℟.

GOSPEL READINGS

1   A reading from the holy gospel
according to Matthew   5:1–12a

Rejoice and be glad, for your reward will be great in heaven.

When he saw the crowds, Jesus went up the mountain, and after
he had sat down, his disciples came to him. He began to teach them,
saying:

    "Blessed are the poor in spirit, for theirs is the kingdom of
      heaven.
    Blessed are they who mourn, for they will be comforted.
    Blessed are the meek, for they will inherit the land.
    Blessed are they who hunger and thirst for righteousness,
      for they will be satisfied.
    Blessed are the merciful, for they will be shown mercy.
    Blessed are the clean of heart, for they will see God.

Blessed are the peacemakers, for they will be called children of
God.

Blessed are they who are persecuted for the sake of righteous-
ness, for theirs is the kingdom of heaven.

Blessed are you when they insult you and persecute you and utter
every kind of evil against you falsely because of me. Rejoice and
be glad, for your reward will be great in heaven."

This is the Gospel of the Lord.

2   A reading from the holy gospel
according to Matthew   11:25–30

Come to me . . . and I will give you rest.

On one occasion Jesus spoke thus: "I give praise to you, Father,
Lord of heaven and earth, for although you have hidden these
things from the wise and the learned you have revealed them to
the childlike. Yes, Father, such has been your gracious will. All
things have been handed over to me by my Father. No one knows
the Son except the Father, and no one knows the Father except
the Son and anyone to whom the Son wishes to reveal him.

"Come to me, all you who labor and are burdened, and I will give
you rest. Take my yoke upon you and learn from me, for I am meek
and humble of heart; and you will find rest for yourselves. For my
yoke is easy, and my burden light."

This is the Gospel of the Lord.

3   A reading from the holy gospel
according to Matthew   25:31-46

Come, you whom my Father has blessed.

Jesus said to his disciples:

"When the Son of Man comes in his glory, and all the angels with
him, he will sit upon his glorious throne, and all the nations will
be assembled before him. And he will separate them one from
another, as a shepherd separates the sheep from the goats. He will
place the sheep on his right and the goats on his left. Then the
king will say to those on his right, 'Come, you who are blessed by
my Father. Inherit the kingdom prepared for you from the foundation of the world. For I was hungry and you gave me food, I

was thirsty and you gave me drink, a stranger and you welcomed me, naked and you clothed me, ill and you cared for me, in prison and you visited me.' Then the righteous will answer him and say, 'Lord, when did we see you hungry and feed you, or thirsty and give you drink? When did we see you a stranger and welcome you, or naked and clothe you? When did we see you ill or in prison, and visit you?' And the king will say to them in reply, 'Amen, I say to you, whatever you did for one of these least brothers of mine, you did for me.'

"Then he will say to those on his left, 'Depart from me, you accursed, into the eternal fire prepared for the devil and his angels. For I was hungry and you gave me no food, I was thirsty and you gave me no drink, a stranger and you gave me no welcome, naked and you gave me no clothing, ill and in prison, and you did not care for me.' Then they will answer and say, 'Lord, when did we see you hungry or thirsty or a stranger or naked or ill or in prison, and not minister to your needs?' He will answer them, 'Amen, I say to you, what you did not do for one of these least ones, you did not do for me.' And these will go off to eternal punishment, but the righteous to eternal life."

This is the Gospel of the Lord.

4   A reading from the holy gospel
    according to Luke   12:35–40

Be prepared.

Jesus said to his disciples:

"Gird your loins and light your lamps and be like servants who await their master's return from a wedding, ready to open immediately when he comes and knocks. Blessed are those servants whom the master finds vigilant on his arrival. Amen, I say to you, he will gird himself, have them recline at table, and proceed to wait on them. And should he come in the second or third watch and find them prepared in this way, blessed are those servants. Be sure of this: if the master of the house had known the hour when the thief was coming, he would not have let his house be broken into. You also must be prepared, for at an hour you do not expect, the Son of Man will come."

This is the Gospel of the Lord.

5   A reading from the holy gospel
     according to Luke   23:33, 39–43

Today you will be with me in paradise.

When they came to the place called the Skull, they crucified Jesus
and the criminals there, one on his right, the other on his left.

Now one of the criminals hanging there reviled Jesus, saying, "Are
you not the Messiah? Save yourself and us." The other, however,
rebuking him, said in reply, "Have you no fear of God, for you are
subject to the same condemnation? And indeed, we have been con-
demned justly, for the sentence we received corresponds to our
crimes, but this man has done nothing criminal." Then he said,
"Jesus, remember me when you come into your kingdom." He re-
plied to him, "Amen, I say to you, today you will be with me in
Paradise."

This is the Gospel of the Lord.

6   A reading from the holy gospel
     according to John   6:37–40

*All who believe in the Son will have eternal life and I will raise
them to life again on the last day.*

Jesus said to the crowd:

"Everything that the Father gives me will come to me, and I will
not reject anyone who comes to me, because I came down from
heaven not to do my own will but the will of the one who sent
me. And this is the will of the one who sent me, that I should not
lose anything of what he gave me, but that I should raise it on the
last day. For this is the will of my Father, that everyone who sees
the Son and believes in him may have eternal life, and I shall raise
him on the last day."

This is the Gospel of the Lord.

7   A reading from the holy gospel
     according to John   11:32–45

Lazarus, come out.

When Mary came to where Jesus was and saw him, she fell at his
feet and said to him, "Lord, if you had been here, my brother would
not have died." When Jesus saw her weeping and the Jews who

had come with her weeping, he became perturbed and deeply troubled, and said, "Where have you laid him?" They said to him, "Sir, come and see." And Jesus wept. So the Jews said, "See how he loved him." But some of them said, "Could not the one who opened the eyes of the blind man have done something so that this man would not have died?"

So Jesus, perturbed again, came to the tomb. It was a cave, and a stone lay across it. Jesus said, "Take away the stone." Martha, the dead man's sister, said to him, "Lord, by now there will be a stench; he has been dead for four days." Jesus said to her, "Did I not tell you that if you believe you will see the glory of God?" So they took away the stone. And Jesus raised his eyes and said, "Father, I thank you for hearing me. I know that you always hear me; but because of the crowd here I have said this, that they may believe that you sent me." And when he had said this, he cried out in a loud voice, "Lazarus, come out!" The dead man came out, tied hand and foot with burial bands, and his face was wrapped in a cloth. So Jesus said to them, "Untie him and let him go."

Now many of the Jews who had come to Mary and seen what he had done began to believe in him.

This is the Gospel of the Lord.

8 A reading from the holy gospel
   according to John   12:23–28

If a grain of wheat falls on the ground and dies, it yields a rich harvest.

Jesus told his disciples:

"The hour has come for the Son of Man to be glorified. Amen, amen, I say to you, unless a grain of wheat falls to the ground and dies, it remains just a grain of wheat; but if it dies, it produces much fruit. Whoever loves his life loses it, and whoever hates his life in this world will preserve it for eternal life. Whoever serves me must follow me, and where I am, there also will my servant be. The Father will honor whoever serves me.

"I am troubled now. Yet what should I say? 'Father, save me from this hour'? But it was for this purpose that I came to this hour. Father, glorify your name." Then a voice came from heaven, "I have glorified it and will glorify it again."

This is the Gospel of the Lord.

9   **A reading from the holy gospel
according to John**   19:17–18, 25–30

Jesus bowed his head and gave up his spirit.

Jesus carrying the cross himself went out to what is called the Place
of the Skull, in Hebrew, Golgotha. There they crucified him, and
with him two others, one on either side, with Jesus in the middle.

Standing by the cross of Jesus were his mother and his mother's
sister, Mary the wife of Clopas, and Mary of Magdala. When Jesus
saw his mother and the disciple there whom he loved, he said to
his mother, "Woman, behold, your son." Then he said to the disciple, "Behold, your mother." And from that hour the disciple took
her into his home.

After this, aware that everything was now finished, in order that
the scripture might be fulfilled, Jesus said, "I thirst." There was a
vessel filled with common wine. So they put a sponge soaked in
wine on a sprig of hyssop and put it up to his mouth. When Jesus
had taken the wine, he said, "It is finished." And bowing his head,
he handed over the spirit.

This is the Gospel of the Lord.

ADDITIONAL TEXTS

Selected Prayers for the Dead

398 The following prayers for the dead may be used in the various rites of the *Order of Christian Funerals.* The prayers should be chosen taking the character of the text into account as well as the place in the rite where it will occur. All of the prayers in this section end with the shorter conclusion.

[The numbers at the right margin refer to the original numbering in the complete edition of the *Order of Christian Funerals.*]

1   General   4

Into your hands, O Lord,
we humbly entrust our brother/sister N.
In this life you embraced him/her with your tender love;
deliver him/her now from every evil
and bid him/her enter eternal rest.
The old order has passed away:
welcome him/her then into paradise,
where there will be no sorrow, no weeping nor pain,
but the fullness of peace and joy
with your Son and the Holy Spirit
for ever and ever.

℟   Amen.

2   General   7

Almighty God and Father,
by the mystery of the cross, you have made us strong;
by the sacrament of the resurrection
you have sealed us as your own.
Look kindly upon your servant N.,
now freed from the bonds of mortality,
and count him/her among your saints in heaven.
We ask this through Christ our Lord.

℟   Amen.

3   General   8

God of loving kindness,
listen favorably to our prayers:
strengthen our belief that your Son has risen from the dead
and our hope that your servant N. will also rise again.
We ask this through Christ our Lord.

℟ Amen.

4   General   10

Lord God, in whom all find refuge,
we appeal to your boundless mercy:
grant to the soul of your servant N.
a kindly welcome,
cleansing of sin,
release from the chains of death,
and entry into everlasting life.
We ask this through Christ our Lord.

℟ Amen.

5   General   11

God of all consolation,
open our hearts to your word,
so that, listening to it, we may comfort one another,
finding light in time of darkness
and faith in time of doubt.
We ask this through Christ our Lord.

℟ Amen.

6   General   13

O God,
in whom sinners find mercy and the saints find joy,
we pray to you for our brother/sister N.,
whose body we honor with Christian burial,
that he/she may be delivered from the bonds of death.
Admit him/her to the joyful company of your saints
and raise him/her on the last day
to rejoice in your presence for ever.
We ask this through Christ our Lord.

℟ Amen.

7 A diocesan bishop 15

Almighty and merciful God,
eternal Shepherd of your people,
listen to our prayers
and grant that your servant, N., our bishop,
to whom you entrusted the care of this Church,
may enter the joy of his eternal Master,
there to receive the rich reward of his labors.
We ask this through Christ our Lord.

℟ Amen.

8 Another bishop 16

O God,
from the ranks of your priests
you chose your servant N.
to fulfill the office of bishop.
Grant that he may share
in the eternal fellowship of those priests
who, faithful to the teachings of the apostles,
dwell in your heavenly kingdom.
We ask this through Christ our Lord.

℟ Amen.

9 A priest 19

Lord God,
you chose our brother N. to serve your people as a priest
and to share the joys and burdens of their lives.
Look with mercy on him
and give him the reward of his labors,
the fullness of life promised to those who preach your
    holy Gospel.
We ask this through Christ our Lord.

℟ Amen.

10 A deacon 21

Lord God,
you sent your Son into the world
to preach the Good News of salvation

and to pour out his Spirit of grace upon your Church.
Look with kindness on your servant N.
As a deacon in the Church
he was strengthened by the gift of the Spirit
to preach the Good News,
to minister in your assembly,
and to do the works of charity.
Give him the reward promised
to those who show their love of you
by service to their neighbor.
We ask this through Christ our Lord.

℟ Amen.

11   A religious   22

All-powerful God,
we pray for our brother/sister N.,
who responded to the call of Christ
and pursued wholeheartedly the ways of perfect love.
Grant that he/she may rejoice
on that day when your glory will be revealed
and in company with all his/her brothers and sisters
share for ever the happiness of your kingdom.
We ask this through Christ our Lord.

℟ Amen.

12   One who worked in the service of the Gospel   24

Faithful God,
we humbly ask your mercy for your servant N.,
who worked so generously to spread the Good News:
grant him/her the reward of his/her labors
and bring him/her safely to your promised land.
We ask this through Christ our Lord.

℟ Amen.

13   A baptized child   26

To you, O Lord,
we humbly entrust this child,

so precious in your sight.
Take him/her into your arms
and welcome him/her into paradise,
where there will be no sorrow, no weeping nor pain,
but the fullness of peace and joy
with your Son and the Holy Spirit
for ever and ever.

℟ Amen.

14   A young person   28

Lord God,
source and destiny of our lives,
in your loving providence
you gave us N.
to grow in wisdom, age, and grace.
Now you have called him/her to yourself.
As we grieve the loss of one so young,
we seek to understand your purpose.
Draw him/her to yourself
and give him/her full stature in Christ.
May he/she stand with all the angels and saints,
who know your love and praise your saving will.
We ask this through Christ our Lord.

℟ Amen.

15   A parent   30

God of our ancestors in faith,
by the covenant made on Mount Sinai
you taught your people to strengthen the bonds of family
through faith, honor, and love.
Look kindly upon N.,
a father/mother who sought to bind his/her children to you.
Bring him/her one day to our heavenly home
where the saints dwell in blessedness and peace.
We ask this through Christ our Lord.

℟ Amen.

16   A married couple 31

Lord God, whose covenant is everlasting,
have mercy upon the sins of your servants N. and N.;
as their love for each other united them on earth,
so let your love join them together in heaven.
We ask this through Christ our Lord.

R⁊ Amen.

17   A wife 34

Eternal God,
you made the union of man and woman
a sign of the bond between Christ and the Church.
Grant mercy and peace to N.,
who was united in love with her husband.
May the care and devotion of her life on earth
find a lasting reward in heaven.
Look kindly on her husband and family/children
as now they turn to your compassion and love.
Strengthen their faith and lighten their loss.
We ask this through Christ our Lord.
R⁊. Amen.

18   A husband 35

Eternal God,
you made the union of man and woman
a sign of the bond between Christ and the Church.
Grant mercy and peace to N.,
who was united in love with his wife.
May the care and devotion of his life on earth
find a lasting reward in heaven.
Look kindly on his wife and family/children
as now they turn to your compassion and love.
Strengthen their faith and lighten their loss.
We ask this through Christ our Lord.
R⁊. Amen.

19   A deceased non-Christian married to a Catholic 36

Almighty and faithful Creator,
all things are of your making,

all people are shaped in your image.
We now entrust the soul of N. to your goodness.
In your infinite wisdom and power,
work in him/her your merciful purpose,
known to you alone from the beginning of time.
Console the hearts of those who love him/her
in the hope that all who trust in you
will find peace and rest in your kingdom.
We ask this in the name of Jesus the Lord.

R⁊ Amen.

20   An elderly person   38

God of mercy,
look kindly on your servant N.
who has set down the burden of his/her years.
As he/she served you faithfully throughout his/her life,
may you give him/her the fullness of your peace and joy.
We give thanks for the long life of N.,
now caught up in your eternal love.
We make our prayer in the name of Jesus who is our risen Lord
now and for ever.

R⁊ Amen.

21   One who died after a long illness   39

God of deliverance,
you called our brother/sister N.
to serve you in weakness and pain,
and gave him/her the grace of sharing the cross of your Son.
Reward his/her patience and forbearance,
and grant him/her the fullness of Christ's victory.
We ask this through Christ our Lord.

R⁊ Amen.

22   One who died suddenly   42

Lord,
as we mourn the sudden death of our brother/sister,
show us the immense power of your goodness
and strengthen our belief
that N. has entered into your presence.

We ask this through Christ our Lord.

℟ Amen.

23　　One who died accidentally or violently　　43

Lord our God,
you are always faithful and quick to show mercy.
Our brother/sister N.
was suddenly (and violently) taken from us.
Come swiftly to his/her aid,
have mercy on him/her,
and comfort his/her family and friends
by the power and protection of the cross.
We ask this through Christ our Lord.

℟ Amen.

24　　One who died by suicide　　44

God, lover of souls,
you hold dear what you have made
and spare all things, for they are yours.
Look gently on your servant N.,
and by the blood of the cross
forgive his/her sins and failings.

Remember the faith of those who mourn
and satisfy their longing for that day
when all will be made new again
in Christ, our risen Lord,
who lives and reigns with you for ever and ever.

℟. Amen.

25　　Several persons　　46

O Lord,
you gave new life to N. and N.
in the waters of baptism;
show mercy to them now,
and bring them to the happiness of life in your kingdom.
We ask this through Christ our Lord.

℟ Amen.

Selected Prayers for the Mourners

399   The following prayers for the mourners may be used in the various rites of the *Order of Christian Funerals*. The prayers should be chosen taking the character of the text into account as well as the place in the rite where it will occur.

[The numbers at the right margin refer to the original numbering in the complete edition of the *Order of Christian Funerals*.]

1   General   1

Father of mercies and God of all consolation,
you pursue us with untiring love
and dispel the shadow of death
with the bright dawn of life.

[Comfort your family in their loss and sorrow.
Be our refuge and our strength, O Lord,
and lift us from the depths of grief
into the peace and light of your presence.]

Your Son, our Lord Jesus Christ,
by dying has destroyed our death,
and by rising, restored our life.
Enable us therefore to press on toward him,
so that, after our earthly course is run,
he may reunite us with those we love,
when every tear will be wiped away.

We ask this through Christ our Lord.

℞. Amen.

2   General   5

Lord God,
you are attentive to the voice of our pleading.
Let us find in your Son
comfort in our sadness,
certainty in our doubt,
and courage to live through this hour.
Make our faith strong
through Christ our Lord.

℞ Amen.

General

Most merciful God,
whose wisdom is beyond our understanding,
surround the family of N. with your love,
that they may not be overwhelmed by their loss,
but have confidence in your goodness,
and strength to meet the days to come.
We ask this through Christ our Lord.

℟   Amen.

A baptized child

Eternal Father,
through the intercession of Mary,
who bore your Son and stood by the cross as he died,
grant to these parents in their grief
the assistance of her presence,
the comfort of her faith,
and the reward of her prayers.
We ask this through Christ our Lord.

℟   Amen.

A baptized child

Lord God,
source and destiny of our lives,
in your loving providence
you gave us N.
to grow in wisdom, age, and grace.
Now you have called him/her to yourself.
We grieve over the loss of one so young
and struggle to understand your purpose.
Draw him/her to yourself
and give him/her full stature in Christ.
May he/she stand with all the angels and saints,
who know your love and praise your saving will.
We ask this through Jesus Christ, our Lord.

℟   Amen.

A child who died before baptism

God of all consolation,
searcher of mind and heart,
the faith of these parents [N. and N.] is known to you.
Comfort them with the knowledge
that the child for whom they grieve
is entrusted now to your loving care.
We ask this through Christ our Lord.

℞ Amen.

7   A stillborn child

Lord God,
ever caring and gentle,
we commit to your love this little one,
quickened to life for so short a time.
Enfold him/her in eternal life.
We pray for his/her parents
who are saddened by the loss of their child.
Give them courage
and help them in their pain and grief.
May they all meet one day
in the joy and peace of your kingdom.
We ask this through Christ our Lord.

℞ Amen.

SELECTED GENERAL INTERCESSIONS AND LITANIES

401 The following intercessions and litanies may be used during a liturgy of the word and should be adopted according to the circumstances.

[The numbers at the right margin refer to the original numbering in the complete edition of the *Order of Christian Funerals.*]

1

1   God, the almighty Father, raised Christ his Son from the dead; with confidence we ask him to save all his people, living and dead:

For N. who in baptism was given the pledge of eternal life, that he/she now be admitted to the company of the saints.
We pray to the Lord.

℟. Lord, hear our prayer.

[For a layperson: For our brother/sister who ate the body of Christ, the bread of life, that he/she may be raised up on the last day.
We pray to the Lord.

℟. Lord, hear our prayer.]

[For a deacon: For our brother N., who proclaimed the Good News of Jesus Christ and served the needs of the poor, that he may be welcomed into the sanctuary of heaven.
We pray to the Lord.

℟. Lord, hear our prayer.]

[For a bishop or priest: For our brother N., who served the Church as a bishop/priest, that he may be given a place in the liturgy of heaven.
We pray to the Lord.

℟. Lord, hear our prayer.]

[For the mourners: For the family and friends of our brother/sister N., that they may be consoled in their grief by the Lord who wept at the death of his friend Lazarus.
We pray to the Lord.

℟. Lord, hear our prayer.]

For our deceased relatives and friends and for all who have helped us, that they may have the reward of their goodness.
We pray to the Lord.

℟. Lord, hear our prayer.

For those who have fallen asleep in the hope of rising again, that they may see God face to face.
We pray to the Lord.

℟. Lord, hear our prayer.

For all of us assembled here to worship in faith, that we may be gathered together again in God's kingdom.
We pray to the Lord.

℟. Lord, hear our prayer.

God, our shelter and our strength,
you listen in love to the cry of your people:
hear the prayers we offer for our departed brothers and sisters.
Cleanse them of their sins
and grant them the fullness of redemption.
We ask this through Christ our Lord.

℞. Amen.

2 My dear friends, let us join with one another in praying to God,
not only for our departed brother/sister, but also for the Church,
for a peace in the world, and for ourselves.

That the bishops priests of the Church, and all who preach the
Gospel, may be given the strength to express in action the word
they proclaim.
We pray to the Lord:

℞. Lord, hear our prayer.

That those in public office may promote justice and peace.
We pray to the Lord:

℞. Lord, hear our prayer.

That those who bear the cross of pain in mind or body may never
feel forsaken by God.
We pray to the Lord:

℞. Lord, hear our prayer.

That God may deliver the soul of his servant N. from punishment
and from the powers of darkness.
We pray to the Lord:

℞. Lord, hear our prayer.

That God in his mercy may blot out all his/her offenses.
We pray to the Lord:

℞. Lord, hear our prayer.

That God may establish him/her in light and peace.
We pray to the Lord:

℞. Lord, hear our prayer.

That God may call him/her to happiness in the company of all the saints. We pray to the Lord:

℟. Lord, hear our prayer.

That God may welcome into his glory those of our family and friends who have departed this life.
We pray to the Lord:

℟. Lord, hear our prayer.

That God may give a place in the kingdom of heaven to all the faithful departed.
We pray to the Lord:

℟. Lord, hear our prayer.

O God,
Creator and Redeemer of all the faithful,
grant to the souls of your departed servants
release from all their sins.
Hear our prayers for those we love
and give them the pardon they have always desired.
We ask this through Christ our Lord.

℟. Amen.

3   A baptized child   5

Jesus is the Son of God and the pattern for our own creation. His promise is that one day we shall truly be like him. With our hope founded on that promise, we pray:

That God will receive our praise and thanksgiving for the life of N.:
Let us pray to the Lord.

℟. Lord, have mercy.

That God will bring to completion N.'s baptism into Christ:
Let us pray to the Lord.

℟. Lord, have mercy.

That God will lead N. from death to life:
Let us pray to the Lord.

℟. Lord, have mercy.

That all of us, N.'s family and friends, may be comforted in our grief:
Let us pray to the Lord.

℞. Lord, have mercy.

That God will grant release to those who suffer:
Let us pray to the Lord.

℞. Lord, have mercy.

That God will grant peace to all who have died in the faith of Christ:
Let us pray to the Lord.

℞. Lord, have mercy.

That one day we may all share in the banquet of the Lord, praising God for victory over death:
Let us pray to the Lord.

℞. Lord, have mercy.

4   A deceased child   7

Let us pray for N., his/her family and friends, and for all God's people.

For N., child of God [and heir to the kingdom], that he/she be held securely in God's loving embrace now and for all eternity.
We pray to the Lord.

℞. Lord, hear our prayer.

For N.'s family, especially his/her mother and father, [his/her brother(s) and sister(s)], that they feel the healing power of Christ in the midst of their pain and grief.
We pray to the Lord.

℞. Lord, hear our prayer.

For N.'s friends, those who played with him/her and those who cared for him/her, that they be consoled in their loss and strengthened in their love for one another.
We pray to the Lord.

℞. Lord, hear our prayer.

For all parents who grieve over the death of their children, that they be comforted in the knowledge that their children dwell with God.
We pray to the Lord.

R⁷. Lord, hear our prayer.

For children who have died of hunger and disease, that these little ones be seated close to the Lord at his heavenly table.
We pray to the Lord.

R⁷. Lord, hear our prayer.

For the whole Church, that we prepare worthily for the hour of our death, when God will call us by name to pass from this world to the next.
We pray to the Lord.

R⁷. Lord, hear our prayer.

Lord God,
you entrusted N. to our care
and now you embrace him/her in your love.
Take N. into your keeping
together with all children who have died.
Comfort us, your sorrowing servants,
who seek to do your will
and to know your saving peace.
We ask this through Christ our Lord.

R⁷. Amen.

MUSIC SUPPLEMENT

Be Not Afraid

*In the first edition of *Glory and Praise*, this phrase appeared as "to foreign men and they."

(Verses)

2 If you pass through rag-ing 2 wa-ters in the sea, you shall not drown. If you 2 walk a-mid the burn-ing flames, you shall not be harmed. If you 2 stand be-fore the pow'r of hell and death is at your side,

Words: Based on Is 43:2-3 and Luke 6:20ff. Robert J. Dufford, s.j.
Music: Robert J. Dufford, s.j., arr. Sister Theophane Hytrek, o.s.f.
Copyright ©1975 by Robert J. Dufford, s.j. and North American Liturgy Resources,
    10802 North 23rd Avenue, Phoenix, Arizona 85029. All rights reserved. Used with permission.

The Cry of the Poor

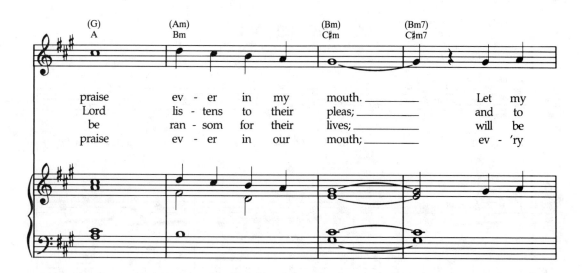

praise ev - er in my mouth. _____ Let my
Lord lis - tens to their pleas; _____ and to
be ran - som for their lives; _____ will be
praise ev - er in our mouth; _____ ev - 'ry

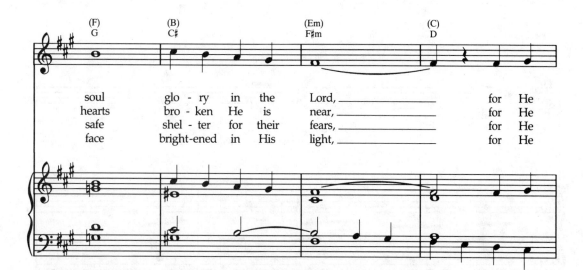

soul glo - ry in the Lord, _____ for He
hearts bro - ken He is near, _____ for He
safe shel - ter for their fears, _____ for He
face bright-ened in His light, _____ for He

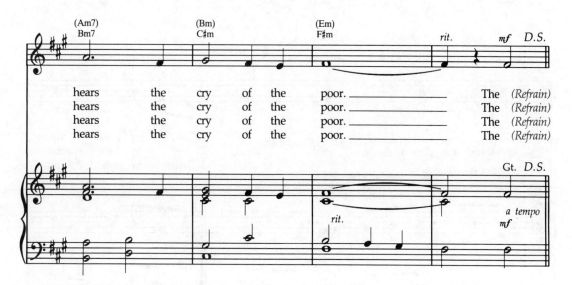

hears the cry of the poor. _____ The (Refrain)
hears the cry of the poor. _____ The (Refrain)
hears the cry of the poor. _____ The (Refrain)
hears the cry of the poor. _____ The (Refrain)

Come to Me

ANTIPHON

♩. = 40

Come to me, all you who thirst: Come, and life shall be yours. Seek and you will find, knock and the door shall be o - pened.

VERSES (for equal voices)

1 Take my yoke up -
2 Seek in faith the
3 Trust in me and

on you and you will find rest for your souls.
King - dom, and all will be giv-en to you.
fear not: Come, drink from the foun-tain of life.

Words: Mt 6:33, 7:7, 11:29; Jn 4:14, 7:37-38
Music: Becket Senchur, O.S.B.

Eye Has Not Seen

spir - it of love, come give us the mind of Je - sus,

teach us the wis - dom of God. _____

(to verses)

(to verses)

VERSES

Melody

Harmony

1 When pain and sor - row weigh us down, be near to us, oh
2 Our lives are but a sin - gle breath, we flow - er and we
3 To those who see with eyes of faith, the Lord is ev - er

1 Lord, for - give the weak-ness of our faith, and bear us up with -
2 face, yet all our days are in your hands, so we re-turn in
3 near, re - flec-ted in the fa - ces, of all the poor and

1 in your peace-ful word. _____
2 love what love has made. _____
3 low - ly of the world. _____

(to refrain)

(to refrain)

VERSE 4

Melody

Harmony

4 We sing a mys - t'ry from the past, in halls where saints have

4 trod, yet ev - er new the mu - sic rings, to Je - sus, liv - ing

Words: Based on 1 Cor. 2:9, 10
Music: Marty Haugen
Copyright ©1982, G.I.A. Publications, Inc. All rights reserved.

Psalm 27: The Lord Is My Light

ANTIPHON

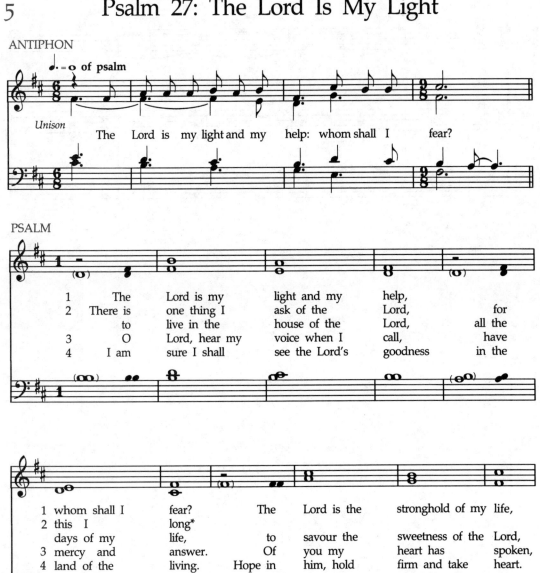

Unison

The Lord is my light and my help: whom shall I fear?

PSALM

1 The Lord is my light and my help,
2 There is one thing I ask of the Lord, for
  to live in the house of the Lord, all the
3 O Lord, hear my voice when I call, have
4 I am sure I shall see the Lord's goodness in the

1 whom shall I fear? The Lord is the stronghold of my life,
2 this I long*
  days of my life, to savour the sweetness of the Lord,
3 mercy and answer. Of you my heart has spoken,
4 land of the living. Hope in him, hold firm and take heart.

1 before whom shall I shrink?
2 to be - hold his [   ] tem - ple.
3 "Seek his face."
4 Hope in the Lord!

*In verse 2, repeat from the beginning ("to live. . .").

Words: Translation of psalm copyright ©1963, The Grail (England). Used with permission.
Music: Joseph Gelineau, copyright ©1963, The Grail (England)

Psalm 42: Like the Deer That Yearns

REFRAIN 1

My soul is thirst-ing for the Lord: when shall I see him face to face?

PSALM

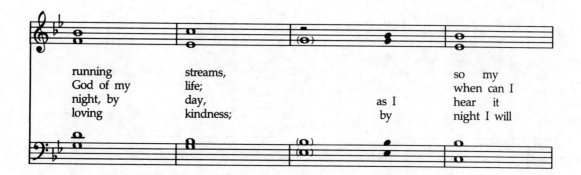

1   Like the deer that yearns   for
2 My   soul is thirsting for God,   the
3 My   tears have be - come my bread,   by
4 By   day the Lord will send   his

running   streams,   so my
God of my   life;   when can I
night, by   day,   as I   hear it
loving   kindness;   by   night I will

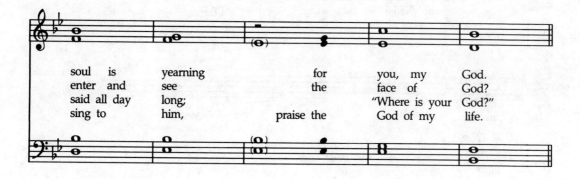

soul is   yearning   for   you, my God.
enter and   see   the   face of God?
said all day   long;   "Where is your God?"
sing to   him,   praise the   God of my life.

Psalm 63: In the Shadow of Your Wings

Psalm 63: My Soul Is Thirsting

My soul is thirst-ing for you, O

Lord, thirst-ing for you my God.

Ps. 62(63), 2. 3-4. 5-6. 8-9

1   O   God, you are my   God, for you I   long;
2   So I   gaze on   you in the   sanctuary
3   So I will   bless you   all my   life,
4   For   you have   been my   help;

for   you my   soul is   thirsting.
to   see your   strength and your   glory.
in your   name I will   lift up my   hands.
in the   shadow of your   wings I re-   joice.

My · body · pines for · you
For your · love is · better than · life,
My · soul shall be · filled as with a · banquet,
My · soul · clings to · you;

like a · dry, weary · land without · water.
my · lips will · speak your · praise.
my · mouth shall · praise you with · joy.
your · right hand · holds me · fast.

Alternate melody for verses:

Words: English translation of the refrain from the *Lectionary for Mass*, copyright ©1969, ICEL.
  Translation of psalm copyright ©1963, The Grail (England). Used with permission.
Music: Refrain by Richard Proulx; psalm setting by Joseph Gelineau.

You Are Near

ANTIPHON

Peacefully (♩=80)

Yah - weh, I know You are near, stand-ing al - ways at my side.

You guard me from the foe, and You

VERSES 2 and 4

2 Where can I run from Your love? If I
4 Mar - vel - ous to me are Your works; how pro -

2 climb to the hea - vens, You are there; If I
4 found are Your thoughts, my Lord. E - ven

2 fly to the sun - rise or sail be - yond the sea,
4 if I could count them, they num - ber as the stars,

2 still I'd find You there. *(Antiphon)*
4 You would still be there. *(Antiphon)*

Words: Based on Psalm 139. Daniel Schutte, s.j.
Music: Daniel Schutte, s.j.

Abide with Me

1 A - bide with me, fast falls the e - ven - tide.
2 I need thy pres - ence ev - 'ry pass - ing hour;
3 Swift to its close ebbs out life's lit - tle day;
4 I fear no foe, with thee at hand to bless;

The dark - ness deep - ens; Lord, with me a - bide.
What but thy grace can foil the tempt - er's pow'r?
Earth's joys grow dim, its glo - ries pass a - way;
Ills have no weight, and tears no bit - ter - ness.

When oth - er help - ers fail and com - forts flee,
Who like thy - self my guide and stay can be?
Change and de - cay in all a - round I see;
Where is death's sting? Where, grave, thy vic - to - ry?

Help of the help - less, oh, a - bide with me.
Through cloud and sun - shine, oh, a - bide with me.
O thou who chang - est not, a - bide with me.
I tri - umph still if thou a - bide with me.

Text: Henry F. Lyte, 1793–1847
Tune: EVENTIDE 10.10.10.10, William H. Monk, 1823–1889

Amazing Grace

(Lower key at number 15B)

1 A - maz - ing grace! How sweet the sound,
2 'Twas grace that taught my heart to fear,
3 The Lord has prom - ised good to me,
4 Through man - y dan - gers, toils, and snares,

That saved and strength - ened me! _____
And grace my fears re - lieved; _____
His word my hope se - cures _____
I have al - read - y come; _____

I once was lost, but now am found,
How pre - cious did that grace ap - pear
He will my shield and por - tion be
'Tis grace hath brought me safe thus far,

Was blind, but now I see. _____
The hour I first be - lieved! _____
As long as life en - dures. _____
And grace will lead me home. _____

Text: John Newton, 1725–1807
Tune: AMAZING GRACE, C.M. Early American melody, arr. by Edwin Othello Excell, 1851–1921.

Merciful Savior

1 Mer - ci - ful Sav - ior, Lord of cre - a - tion,
2 Mer - ci - ful Sav - ior, King of the na - tions,

Son of God and Son of Man!
Son of God and Son of Man!

Je - sus, we love you, Serve and o - bey you,
Glo - ry and hon - or, Praise, ad - o - ra - tion,

Light of the soul, our joy and peace.
Ev - er be yours from all man - kind!

Text: Irwin Udulutsch, o.f.m. cap., copyright ©1959, 1977, The Order of St. Benedict, Inc.
Tune: ST. ELIZABETH, Irreg., *Schlesische Volkslieder*, 1842

Day Is Done

Capo 3; play D

1 Day is done, but Love un-fail-ing Dwells ev-er here;
2 Dark de-scends, but Light un-end-ing Shines through our night;
3 Eyes will close, but you un-sleep-ing Watch by our side;

Shad-ows fall, but hope pre-vail-ing Calms ev-'ry fear.
You are with us, ev-er lend-ing New strength to sight:
Death may come, in Love's safe-keep-ing Still we a-bide.

Lov-ing Fa-ther, none for-sak-ing, Take our hearts, of
One in love, your truth con-fess-ing, One in hope of
God of love, all e-vil quell-ing, Sin for-giv-ing,

Love's own mak-ing, Watch our sleep-ing, guard our wak-ing, Be al-ways near.
heav-en's bless-ing, May we see, in love's pos-sess-ing, Love's end-less light!
fear dis-pell-ing, Stay with us, our hearts in-dwell-ing, This e-ven-tide.

Text: James Quinn, s.j., b. 1919, copyright ©James Quinn, s.j.
Reprinted by permission of Geoffrey Chapman, a division of Cassell, Ltd., 1 Vincent Square, London SW1P 2PN.
Tune: AR HYD Y NOS, 84.84.888.4, Welsh Tune. Setting from *The English Hymnal*, copyright ©Oxford University Press.
Used with permission. Not for sale outside the U.S.A.

How Great Thou Art

Capo 3; play G

1 O Lord, my God! When I in awe-some won-der Con-sid-er
2 When Christ shall come with shout of ac-cla - ma - tion And take me

all the worlds* thy hands have made, I see the stars, I hear the roll-ing*
home, what joys shall fill my heart! Then I shall bow in hum-ble ad-o -

thun - der, Thy pow'r through-out the u - ni-verse dis - played,
ra - tion And there pro - claim, my God, how great thou art!

REFRAIN

Then sings my soul, my Sav - ior God, to thee. How great thou

*Author's original words are "works" and "mighty".

I Call You to My Father's House

1 I call you to my Fa - ther's house, A love - ly dwell - ing place. He comes to meet you on the road, Arms read - y to em - brace.

2 Lay down your sor - row, calm your fear; The Fa - ther bids you come. With o - pen arms He wel-comes you To your e - ter - nal home.

3 Al - though the way be hard and long In - to the prom - ised land, Be not a - fraid to walk with Me: I hold you by the hand.

4 I have pre - pared a wed - ding feast Of fin - est food and wine. O join us at this ban - quet where My friends, the saints, now dine.

5 I call you to my Fa - ther's house, A love - ly dwell - ing place. Be not a - fraid to trav - el there And meet Him face to face.

The above text may be sung to familiar melodies on the following page:
AMAZING GRACE
LAND OF REST (Jerusalem, My Happy Home).

Text: Delores Dufner, O.S.B., copyright © 1983, the Sisters of St. Benedict, St. Joseph, Minn., 56374
Tune: 87.87, copyright ©1983, Jay Hunstiger, 4545 Wichita Trail, Medina, Minn. 55340

I Call You to My Father's House

(Alternate tune)

(Higher key at number 17)

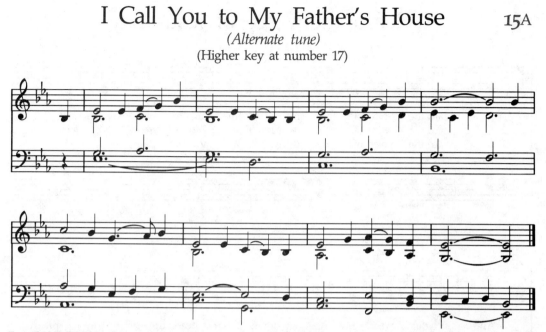

Tune: LAND OF REST, C.M., trad. American melody, acc. by Sister Theophane Hytrek, O.S.F., copyright ©1980, ICEL

I Call You to My Father's House

(Alternate Tune)

(Higher key at numbers 11 and 24)

Tune: AMAZING GRACE, C.M., early American melody, arr. by Edwin Othello Excell, 1851–1921

I Heard the Voice of Jesus Say

1 I heard the voice of Je - sus say, "Come un - to me and rest;
2 I heard the voice of Je - sus say, "Be - hold, I free - ly give
3 I heard the voice of Je - sus say, "I am this dark world's light;

And in your wear - i - ness lay down Your head up - on my breast."
The liv - ing wa - ter thirst - y one: Stoop down and drink and live."
Look un - to me, your morn shall rise, And all your day be bright."

I came to Je - sus and I was, So wear - y, worn, and sad;
I came to Je - sus and I drank Of that life - giv - ing stream;
I looked to Je - sus and I found In him my star, my sun;

I found in him a rest - ing place, And he has made me glad.
My thirst was quenched, my soul re - vived, And now I live in him.
and in that light of life I'll walk Till all my days are done.

Text: Horatius Bonar, 1808–1889
Tune: KINGSFOLD, harm. and arr. by Ralph Vaughan Williams, 1872–1958,
    setting from *The English Hymnal*, copyright ©Oxford University Press. Not for sale outside the U.S.A.

Jerusalem, My Happy Home

(Lower key at number 15A)

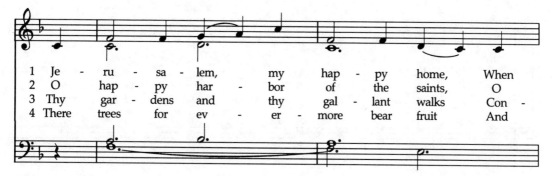

1 Je - ru - sa - lem, my hap - py home, When
2 O hap - py har - bor of the saints, O
3 Thy gar - dens and thy gal - lant walks Con -
4 There trees for ev - er - more bear fruit And

shall I come to thee? When shall my sor - rows
sweet and pleas - ant soil! In thee no sor - row
tin - ual - ly are green; There grow such sweet and
ev - er - more do spring; There ev - er - more the

have an end? Thy joys when shall I see?
may be found, No grief, no care, no toil.
pleas - ant flow'rs As no - where else are seen.
an - gels sit And ev - er - more do sing.

5 Jerusalem, Jerusalem,
God grant that I may see
Thine endless joy, and of the same
Partaker ever be!

Text: F.B.P. in the *Song of Mary*, 1601
Tune: LAND OF REST, C.M., trad. American melody, acc. by Sister Theophane Hytrek, o.s.f., 1980, copyright ©1980, ICEL

Lord Jesus Christ, Abide with Us

18

1 Lord Jesus Christ, abide with us,
Now that the sun has run its course;
Let hope not be obscured by night,
But may faith's darkness be as light.

2 Lord Jesus Christ, grant us your peace,
And when the trials of earth shall cease,
Grant us the morning light of grace,
The radiant splendor of your face.

3 Immortal, Holy, Threefold Light,
Yours be the kingdom, pow'r, and might;
All glory be eternally,
To you, life-giving Trinity.

Text: *Mane nobiscum Domine*, paraphrased by Jerome Leaman, copyright ©Jerome Leaman
Tune: OLD HUNDREDTH, L.M., Louis Bourgeois, c. 1510–1561

1 The King of love my shepherd is,
2 Where streams of living water flow
3 Perverse and foolish I have strayed
4 In death's dark vale I fear no ill

Whose goodness fails me never;
With gentle care he leads me,
But yet in love he sought me,
With you, dear Lord, beside me,

I nothing lack if I am his,
And where the verdant pastures grow
And on his shoulder gently laid,
Your rod and staff my comfort still,

And he is mine for ever.
With heav'nly food he feeds me.
And home, rejoicing, brought me.
Your Cross before to guide me.

5 You spread a table in my sight,
  Your saving grace bestowing;
  And O what joy and true delight
  From your pure chalice flowing!

6 And so through all the length of days
  Your goodness fails me never;
  Good Shepherd, may I sing your praise
  Within your house for ever.

Text: Based on Ps. 22, Matt. 18, and Jn. 10, Sir Henry Williams Baker, 1821–1877
Tune: ST. COLUMBA (ERIN), 87.87, trad. Irish hymn melody. Acc. by Russell Woollen, 1980, copyright ©1980, ICEL

The King Shall Come

1 The King shall come when morn-ing dawns And light tri-um-phant breaks,
2 Not as of old a lit-tle child To bear and fight and die,
3 Oh, bright-er than the ris-ing morn When Christ, vic-to-rious, rose
4 Oh, bright-er than that glo-rious morn Shall dawn up-on our race

When beau-ty gilds the east-ern hills And life to joy a-wakes.
But crowned with glo-ry like the sun That lights the morn-ing sky.
And left the lone-some place of death, De-spite the rage of foes.
The day when Christ in splen-dor comes, And we shall see his face.

Text: John Brownlie, 1859–1925, alt.
Tune: CONSOLATION (MORNING HYMN), C.M., A. Davisson, *Kentucky Harmony*, 1816,
    harm. Charles Winfred Douglas 1867–1944

There's a Wideness in God's Mercy

1 There's a wide-ness in God's mer - cy, Like the wide-ness of the sea;
2 For the love of God is broad - er Than the meas-ure of man's mind;

There's a kind-ness in his jus - tice, Which is more than lib - er - ty.
And the heart of the E - ter-nal Is most won-der - ful -ly kind.

There is wel-come for the sin - ner, And more bless - ings for the good;
There is plen - ti - ful re - demp-tion In the blood that has been shed;

There is mer - cy with the Sav - ior; There is heal-ing in his blood.
There is joy for all the mem - bers Now at one with Christ our Head.

Text: Frederick William Faber, 1814–1863, alt.
Tune: 87.87.D, Gerard Wojchowski, o.s.b., copyright ©1965, 1977, The Order of St. Benedict, Inc., Collegeville, Minn.

O God, Our Help in Ages Past

1 O God, our help in ages past,
2 Be - neath the shad - ow of thy throne Thy
3 Be - fore the hills in or - der stood, Or
4 A thou - sand a - ges in thy sight Are

hope for years to come, Our shel - ter from the
saints have dwelt se - cure; Suf - fi - cient is thine
earth re - ceived her frame, From ev - er - last - ing
like an eve - ning gone: Short as the watch that

storm - y blast, And our e - ter - nal home!
arm a - lone, And our de - fence is sure.
thou art God, To end - less years the same.
ends the night Be - fore the ri - sing sun.

5 O God, our help in ages past,
Our hope for years to come;
Be thou our guard while troubles last,
And our eternal home!

Text: Based on Psalm 90(89), Isaac Watts, 1674–1748
Tune: ST. ANNE, C.M., attr. to William Croft, 1678–1727

O Glorify the Lord

1 O glo-ri-fy the Lord with me! To-geth-er let us praise his name.
2 The Lord is close to bro-ken hearts: I sought the Lord; he an-swered me.
3 O taste and see the Lord is good! In him is all my heart's de-light.
4 Let ev-'ry crea-ture praise the Lord From north and south, from east and west.

His faith-ful-ness will nev-er end; In ev-'ry age he is the same.
The crushed in spir-it he will save: From all my fears he set me free.
O come and fol-low Christ the Lord, That you may share his glo-ry bright.
In him a-lone we shall find joy; In him a-lone, e-ter-nal rest.

5 At all times let us bless the Lord,
And ever on our lips his praise.
Let us give thanks for mercies past,
And glorify him all our days!

The above text may be sung to the familiar tunes on the following page:
JESU, DULCIS MEMORIA (O Jesus, Joy of Loving Hearts)
OLD HUNDREDTH (Praise God, From Whom All Blessings Flow)

Text: Adapted from Ps. 34, Delores Dufner, O.S.B.,
Copyright ©1982, the Sisters of St. Benedict, St. Joseph, Minn. 56374
Tune: 8.8.8.8., copyright ©1982, Jay Hunstiger, 4545 Wichita Trail, Medina, Minn. 55340

O Glorify the Lord

Alternate Tune

Tune: OLD 100TH, L.M., Louis Bourgeois, c. 1510–1561, in *Genevan Psalter*, 1551

O Glorify the Lord

Alternate Tune

Tune: JESU, DULCIS MEMORIA, L.M., Plainchant, mode I, acc. by Theodore Marier, copyright ©1980, ICEL

Mary's Song

1 My soul proclaims you, mighty God.
2 All nations now will share my joy;
3 For those who love your holy name,
4 You fill the hungry with good things;

My spirit sings your praise.
Your gifts you have outpoured.
Your mercy will not die.
The rich you send away.

You look on me, you lift me up,
Your little one you have made great.
Your strong right arm puts down the proud,
The promise made to Abraham

And gladness fills my days.
I magnify my God.
And lifts the lowly high.
Is filled to endless day.

5 Magnificat, magnificat,
Magnificat, praise God!
Praise God, praise God, praise God, praise God,
Magnificat, praise God!

Text: Sister Anne Carter, R.S.C.J., copyright ©1988, The Religious of the Sacred Heart. Used by permission.
Tune: AMAZING GRACE, C.M. Early American melody, arr. by Edwin Othello Excell, 1851-1921.

My Shepherd Will Supply My Need

1 My Shep - herd will sup - ply my need; The
2 When I walk through the shades of death, Thy
3 The sure pro - vi - sions of my God At -

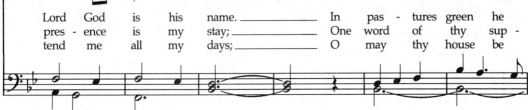

Lord God is his name._____ In pas - tures green he
pres - ence is my stay;_____ One word of thy sup -
tend me all my days;_____ O may thy house be

makes me feed, Be - side the liv - ing stream._____ He
port - ing breath Drives all my fears a - way._____ Thy
my a - bode, And all my work be praise!_____ There

brings my wan - d'ring spir - it back, When I for -
hand, in sight of all my foes, Does still my
would I find a set - tled rest, While oth - ers

sake his ways; _____ And leads me for his
ta - ble spread; _____ My cup with bless - ings
go and come, _____ No more a stran - ger

mer - cy's sake, In paths of truth and grace. _____
o - ver - flows, Thine oil a - noints my head. _____
nor a guest; But like a child at home. _____

Text: Psalm 22(23), Isaac Watts, 1674–1748, alt.
Tune: RESIGNATION, C.M.D., *Southern Harmony*, 1835, acc. by Sister Theophane Hytrek, o.s.f., 1980, copyright ©1980 ICEL

When Nature Has Nestled

1 When na-ture has nes-tled be-neath Your great wings,
2 When life has flowed gen-tly toward beck-on-ing shores,
3 When whis-per-ing pines have ca-ressed wea-ry hearts,

When shad-ows have spilled from the gold-en west,
When days have grown grace-ful-ly in-to years,
When day-dreams have ten-der-ly turned to night,

When the sun sinks and the dark-ness de-scends,
When our eyes close and the dark-ness de-scends,
When all our fears have been soothed by Your touch,

Safe in Your em-brace, Lord, in peace shall we rest.
Safe in Your em-brace, we shall dry all our tears.
Safe in Your em-brace, shall we sleep till the light.

Text: Delores Dufner, o.s.b., copyright ©1983, the Sisters of St. Benedict, St. Joseph, Minn. 56374
Tune: 11.10.10.11, copyright ©1983, Jay Hunstiger, 4545 Wichita Trail, Medina, Minn. 55340

When Nature Has Nestled
Alternate Tune

1 When na - ture has nes - tled be - neath Your great
2 When life has flowed gen - tly toward beck - on - ing
3 When whis - per - ing pines have ca - ressed wea - ry

wings, When shad - ows have spilled from the gold - en
shores, When days have grown grace - ful - ly in - to
hearts, When day - dreams have ten - der - ly turned to

west, Then, when the sun sinks and the dark - ness de -
years, Then, when our eyes close and the dark - ness de -
night, Then, when all our fears have been soothed by Your

scends, Safe in Your em - brace, Lord, in peace shall we rest.
scends, Safe in Your em - brace, we shall dry all our tears.
touch, Safe in Your em - brace, shall we sleep till the light.

Text: Delores Dufner, o.s.b., copyright ©1983, the Sisters of St. Benedict, St. Joseph, Minn. 56374
Tune: FOUNDATION, 11.11.11.11 (alt.), traditional American hymn melody.
  Acc. by Russell Woollen, 1980, copyright ©1980, ICEL

INDEX OF MUSIC PIECES

Responsorial Pieces

Hymns